SPECIAL NEEDS IN ORDINA
General Editor: Peter Mittler

Humanities for All

Special Needs in Ordinary Schools

General editor: Peter Mittler
Associate editors: James Hogg, Peter Pumfrey, Tessa Roberts, Colin Robson
Honorary advisory board: Neville Bennett, Marion Blythman, George Cooke, John Fish, Ken Jones, Sylvia Phillips, Klaus Wedell, Phillip Williams

Titles in this series

Meeting Special Needs in Ordinary Schools: An Overview

Concerning pre- and primary schooling:

Communication in the Primary School
Developing Mathematical and Scientific Thinking in Young Children
Exploring the Environment
Expressive and Creative Skills
Primary Schools and Special Needs: Policy, Planning and Provision
Special Needs in Pre-Schools

Concerning secondary schooling:

Humanities for All: Teaching Humanities in the Secondary School
Responding to Adolescent Needs: A Pastoral Care Approach
Science for All: Teaching Science in the Secondary School
Secondary Schools for All? Strategies for Special Needs
Shut Up! Communication in the Secondary School
Teaching Mathematics in the Secondary School

Concerning specific difficulties:

Children with Learning Difficulties
Children with Speech and Language Difficulties
Making a Difference: Teachers, Pupils and Behaviour
Physically Disabled Children
The Hearing Impaired Child
The Visually Handicapped Child in Your Classroom

Humanities for All:

Teaching Humanities in the Secondary School

John Clarke and Kathryn Wrigley

Cassell

Cassell Educational Limited
Artillery House
Artillery Row
London SW1P 1RT

British Library Cataloguing in Publication Data
Clarke, John
    Humanities for all: teaching humanities
    in the secondary school.—(Special needs
    in ordinary schools)
    1. Great Britain. Secondary schools.
    Curriculum subjects: Humanities.
    Curriculum. Development
    I. Title II. Wrigley, Kathryn III. Series
    001.3'07'1241

ISBN: 0 – 304 – 31398 – X

Typeset by Activity Ltd., Salisbury, Wilts.
Printed and bound in Great Britain by Biddles Ltd.,
Guildford and King's Lynn

First published 1988

Last digit is print no: 9 8 7 6 5 4 3 2 1

Contents

Acknowledgements

We are indebted to many for help in the preparation of this book: to Peter Pumfrey for encouragement and constructive criticism; to NARE for permission to reproduce Colin McCall's work from *Planning Effective Progress*; to Mel Ainscow for an early glimpse of the secondary SNAP materials; to Annie Fergusson for her library facilities and to the staff and pupils of Wardle High School, Rochdale, for their forbearance, particularly that of John Lord, Meg Williams and Steve Cooke.

Most of all we are grateful to Judy Sebba and David Edmonds for continuing professional and personal support.

To Les and Margaret Clarke, and Len and Betty Baxter

Foreword: Towards education for all

AIMS

This series aims to support teachers as they respond to the challenge they face in meeting the needs of all children in their school, particularly those identified as having special educational needs.

Although there have been many useful publications in the field of special educational needs during the last decade, the distinguishing feature of the present series of volumes lies in their concern with specific areas of the curriculum in primary and secondary schools. We have tried to produce a series of conceptually coherent and professionally relevant books, each of which is concerned with ways in which children with varying levels of ability and motivation can be taught together. The books draw on the experience of practising teachers, teacher trainers and researchers and seek to provide practical guidelines on ways in which specific areas of the curriculum can be made more accessible to all children. The volumes provide many examples of curriculum adaptation, class-room activities, teacher–child interactions, as well as the mobilisation of resources inside and outside the school.

The series is organised largely in terms of age and subject groupings, but three 'overview' volumes have been prepared in order to provide an account of some major current issues and developments. Seamus Hegarty's *Meeting Special Needs in Ordinary Schools* gives an introduction to the field of special needs as a whole, whilst Sheila Wolfendale's *Primary Schools and Special Needs* and John Sayer's *Secondary Schools for All?* address issues more specifically concerned with primary and secondary schools respectively. We hope that curriculum specialists will find essential background and contextual material in these overview volumes.

In addition, a section of this series will be concerned with examples of obstacles to learning. All of these specific special needs can be seen on a continuum ranging from mild to severe, or from temporary and transient to long-standing or permanent. These include difficulties in learning or in adjustment and behaviour, as well as problems resulting largely from sensory or physical impairments or from difficulties of communication from whatever cause. We hope that teachers will consult the volumes in this section for guidance on working with children with specific difficulties.

The series aims to make a modest 'distance learning' contribution to meeting the needs of teachers working with the whole range of pupils with special educational needs by offering a set of resource materials relating to specific areas of the primary and secondary curriculum and by suggesting ways in which learning obstacles, whatever their origin, can be identified and addressed.

We hope that these materials will not only be used for private study but be subjected to critical scrutiny by school-based inservice groups sharing common curricular interests and by staff of institutions of higher education concerned with both special needs teaching and specific curriculum areas. The series has been planned to provide a resource for Local Education Authority (LEA) advisers, specialist teachers from all sectors of the education service, educational psychologists, and teacher working parties. We hope that the books will provide a stimulus for dialogue and serve as catalysts for improved practice.

It is our hope that parents will also be encouraged to read about new ideas in teaching children with special needs so that they can be in a better position to work in partnership with teachers on the basis of an informed and critical understanding of current difficulties and developments. The goal of 'Education for All' can only be reached if we succeed in developing a working partnership between teachers, pupils, parents, and the community at large.

ELEMENTS OF A WHOLE-SCHOOL APPROACH

Meeting special educational needs in ordinary schools is much more than a process of opening school doors to admit children previously placed in special schools. It involves a radical re-examination of what all schools have to offer all children. Our efforts will be judged in the long term by our success with children who are already in ordinary schools but whose needs are not being met, for whatever reason.

The additional challenge of achieving full educational as well as social integration for children now in special schools needs to be seen in the wider context of a major reappraisal of what ordinary schools have to offer the pupils already in them. The debate about integration of handicapped and disabled children in ordinary schools should not be allowed to overshadow the movement for curriculum reform in the schools themselves. If successful, this could promote the fuller integration of the children already in the schools.

If this is the aim of current policy, as it is of this series of unit texts, we have to begin by examining ways in which schools and school policies can themselves be a major element in children's difficulties.

Can schools cause special needs?

Traditionally, we have looked for causes of learning difficulty in the child. Children have been subjected to tests and investigations by doctors, psychologists and teachers with the aim of pinpointing the nature of the problem and in the hope that this might lead to specific programmes of teaching and intervention. We less frequently ask ourselves whether what and how we teach and the way in which we organise and manage our schools could themselves be a major cause of children's difficulties.

The shift of emphasis towards a whole-school policy is sometimes described in terms of a move away from the deficit or medical model of special education towards a more environmental or ecological model. Clearly, we are concerned here with an interaction between the two. No one would deny that the origins of some learning difficulties do lie in the child. But even where a clear cause can be established – for example, a child with severe brain damage, or one with a serious sensory or motor disorder – it would be simplistic to attribute all the child's learning difficulties to the basic impairment alone.

The ecological model starts from the position that the growth and development of children can be understood only in relation to the nature of their interactions with the various environments which impinge on them and with which they are constantly interacting. These environments include the home and each individual member of the immediate and extended family. Equally important are other children in the neighbourhood and at school, as well as people with whom the child comes into casual or closer contact. We also need to consider the local and wider community and its various institutions –not least, the powerful influence of television, which for some children represents more hours of information intake than is provided by teachers during eleven years of compulsory education. The ecological model thus describes a gradually widening series of concentric circles, each of which provides a powerful series of influences and possibilities for interaction – and therefore learning.

Schools and schooling are only one of many environmental influences affecting the development and learning of children. A great deal has been learned from other environments before the child enters school and much more will be learned after the child leaves full-time education. Schools represent a relatively powerful series of environments, not all concerned with formal learning. During the hours spent in school, it is hard to estimate the extent to which the number and nature of the interactions experienced by any one child are directly concerned with formal teaching and learning. Social interactions with other children also need to be considered.

Questions concerned with access to the curriculum lie at the heart of any whole-school policy. What factors limit the access of certain children to the curriculum? What modifications are necessary to ensure fuller curriculum access? Are there areas of the curriculum from which some children are excluded? Is this because they are thought 'unlikely to be able to benefit'? And even if they are physically present, are there particular lessons or activities which are inaccessible because textbooks or worksheets demand a level of literacy and comprehension which effectively prevent access? Are there tasks in which children partly or wholly fail to understand the language which the teacher is using? Are some teaching styles inappropriate for individual children?

Is it possible that some learning difficulties arise from the ways in which schools are organised and managed? For example, what messages are we conveying when we separate some children from others? How does the language we use to describe certain children reflect our own values and assumptions? How do schools transmit value judgements about children who succeed and those who do not? In the days when there was talk of comprehensive schools being 'grammar schools for all', what hope was there for children who were experiencing significant learning difficulties? And even today, what messages are we transmitting to children and their peers when we exclude them from participation in some school activities? How many children with special needs will be entered for the new General Certificate of Secondary Education (GCSE) examinations? How many have taken or will take part in Technical and Vocational Education Initiative (TVEI) schemes?

The argument here is not that all children should have access to all aspects of the curriculum. Rather it is a plea for the individualisation of learning opportunities for all children. This requires a broad curriculum with a rich choice of learning opportunities designed to suit the very wide range of individual needs.

Curriculum reform

The last decade has seen an increasingly interventionist approach by Her Majesty's Inspectors of Education (HMI), by officials of the Department of Education and Science (DES) and by individual Secretaries of State. The 'Great Debate', allegedly beginning in 1976, led to a flood of curriculum guidelines from the centre. The garden is secret no longer. Whilst Britain is far from the centrally imposed curriculum found in some other countries, government is increasingly insisting that schools must reflect certain key areas of experience for all pupils, and in particular those concerned with the world of work (*sic*), with science and technology, and with economic awareness. These priorities are also reflected in the prescriptions for teacher education laid down with an increasing degree of firmness from the centre.

There are indications that a major reappraisal of curriculum content and access is already under way and seems to be well supported by teachers. Perhaps the best known and most recent examples can be found in the series of Inner London Education Authority (ILEA) reports concerned with secondary, primary and special education, known as the Hargreaves, Thomas and Fish Reports (ILEA, 1984, 1985a, 1985b). In particular, the Hargreaves Report envisaged a radical reform of the secondary curriculum, based to some extent on his book *Challenge for the Comprehensive School* (Hargreaves, 1982). This envisages a major shift of emphasis from the 'cognitive-academic' curriculum of many secondary schools towards one emphasising more personal involvement by pupils in selecting their own patterns of study from a wider range of choice. If the proposals in these reports were to be even partially implemented, pupils with special needs would stand to benefit from such a wholesale review of the curriculum of the school as a whole.

Pupils with special needs also stand to benefit from other developments in mainstream education. These include new approaches to records of achievement, particularly 'profiling' and a greater emphasis on criterion–referenced assessment. Some caution has already been expressed about the extent to which the new GCSE examinations will reach less able children previously excluded from the Certificate of Secondary Education. Similar caution is justified in relation to the TVEI and the Certificate of Pre-Vocational Education (CPVE). And what about the new training initiatives for school leavers and the 14–19 age group in general? Certainly, the pronouncements of the Manpower Services Commission (MSC) emphasise a policy of provision for all, and have made specific arrangements for young people with special needs, including those with disabilities. In the last analysis, society and its institutions will be judged by their success in preparing the majority of young people to make an effective and valued contribution to the community as a whole.

A CLIMATE OF CHANGE

Despite the very real and sometimes overwhelming difficulties faced by schools and teachers as a result of underfunding and professional unrest, there are encouraging signs of change and reform which, if successful, could have a significant impact not only on children with special needs but on all children. Some of these are briefly mentioned below.

The campaign for equal opportunities

First, we are more aware of the need to confront issues concerned with civil rights and equal opportunities. All professionals concerned with human services are being asked to examine their own attitudes and practices and to question the extent to which these might unwittingly or even deliberately discriminate unfairly against some sections of the population.

We are more conscious than ever of the need to take positive steps to promote the full access of girls and women not only to full educational opportunities but also to the whole range of community resources and services, including employment, leisure, housing, social security and the right to property. We have a similar concern for members of ethnic and religious groups who have been and still are victims of discrimination and restricted opportunities for participation in society and its institutions. It is no accident that the title of the Swann Report on children from ethnic minorities was *Education for All* (Committee of Inquiry, 1985). This too is the theme of the present series and the underlying aim of the movement to meet the whole range of special needs in ordinary schools.

The equal opportunities movement has not itself always fully accepted people with disabilities and special needs. At national level, there is no legislation specifically concerned with discrimination against people with disabilities, though this does exist in some other countries. The Equal Opportunities Commission does not concern itself with disability issues. On the other hand, an increasing number of local authorities and large corporations claim to be 'Equal Opportunities Employers', specifically mentioning disability alongside gender, ethnicity and sexual orientation. Furthermore, the 1986 Disabled Persons Act, arising from a private member's Bill and now on the statute book, seeks to carry forward for adults some of the more positive features of the 1981 Education Act – for example, it provides for the rights of all people with disabilities to take part or be represented in discussion and decision-making concerning services provided for them.

These developments, however, have been largely concerned with children or adults with disabilities, rather than with children already in ordinary schools. Powerful voluntary organisations such as MENCAP (the Royal Society for Mentally Handicapped Children and Adults) and the Spastics Society have helped to raise political and public awareness of the needs of children with disabilities and have fought hard and on the whole successfully to secure better services for them and for their families. Similarly, organisations of adults with disabilities, such as the British Council of Organisations for Disabled People, are pressing hard for better quality, integrated education, given their own personal experiences of segregated provision.

Special needs and social disadvantage

Even these developments have largely bypassed two of the largest groups now in special schools: those with moderate learning difficulties and those with emotional and behavioural difficulties. There are no powerful pressure groups to speak for them, for the same reason that no pressure groups speak for the needs of children with special needs already in ordinary schools. Many of these children come from families which do not readily form themselves into associations and pressure groups. Many of their parents are unemployed, on low incomes or dependent on social security; many live in overcrowded conditions in poor quality housing or have long-standing health problems. Some members of these families have themselves experienced school failure and rejection as children.

Problems of poverty and disadvantage are common in families of children with special needs already in ordinary schools. Low achievement and social disadvantage are clearly associated, though it is important not to assume that there is a simple relation between them. Although most children from socially disadvantaged backgrounds have not been identified as low achieving, there is still a high correlation between social-class membership and educational achievement, with middle-class children distancing themselves increasingly in educational achievements and perhaps also socially from children from working-class backgrounds – another form of segregation within what purports to be the mainstream.

The probability of socially disadvantaged children being identified as having special needs is very much greater than in other children. An early estimate suggested that it was more than seven times as high, when social disadvantage was defined by the presence of all three of the following indices: overcrowding (more than 1.5 persons per room), low income (supplementary benefit or free school meals) and adverse family circumstances (coming from a single-parent home or a home with more than five children) (Wedge and Prosser, 1973). Since this study was published, the number of families coming into these categories has greatly increased as a result of deteriorating economic conditions and changing social circumstances.

In this wider sense, the problem of special needs is largely a problem of social disadvantage and poverty. Children with special needs are therefore doubly vulnerable to underestimation of their abilities: first, because of their family and social backgrounds, and second, because of their low achievements. A recent large-scale study of special needs provision in junior schools suggests that while teachers' attitudes to low-achieving children are broadly positive, they are pessimistic about the ability of such children to derive much benefit from increased special needs provision (Croll and Moses, 1985).

Partnership with parents

The Croll and Moses survey of junior school practice confirms that teachers still tend to attribute many children's difficulties to adverse home circumstances. How many times have we heard comments along the lines of 'What can you expect from a child from that kind of family?' Is this not a form of stereotyping at least as damaging as racist and sexist attitudes?

Partnership with parents of socially disadvantaged children thus presents a very different challenge from that portrayed in the many reports of successful practice in some special schools. Nevertheless, the challenge can be and is being met. Paul Widlake's recent books (1984, 1985) give the lie to the oft-expressed view that some parents are 'not interested in their child's education'. Widlake documents project after project in which teachers and parents have worked well together. Many of these projects have involved teachers visiting homes rather than parents attending school meetings. There is also now ample research to show that children whose parents listen to them reading at home tend to read better and to enjoy reading more than other children (Topping and Wolfendale, 1985; see also Sheila Wolfendale's *Primary Schools and Special Needs*, in the present series).

Support in the classroom

If teachers in ordinary schools are to identify and meet the whole range of special needs, including those of children currently in special schools, they are entitled to support. Above all, this must come from the head teacher and from the senior staff of the school; from any special needs specialists or teams already in the school; from members of the new advisory and support services, as well as from educational psychologists, social workers and any health professionals who may be involved.

This support can take many forms. In the past, support meant removing the child for considerable periods of time into the care of remedial teachers either within the school or coming from outside. Withdrawal now tends to be discouraged, partly because it is thought to be another form of segregation within the ordinary school, and therefore in danger of isolating and stigmatising children, and partly because it deprives children of access to lessons and activities available to other children. In a major survey of special needs provision in middle and secondary schools, Clunies-Ross and Wimhurst (1983) showed that children with special needs were most often withdrawn from science and modern languages in order to find the time to give them extra help with literacy.

Many schools and LEAs are exploring ways in which both teachers and children can be supported without withdrawing children from ordinary classes. For example, special needs teachers increasingly are working alongside their colleagues in ordinary classrooms, not just with a small group of children with special needs but also with all children. Others are working as consultants to their colleagues in discussing the level of difficulty demanded of children following a particular course or specific lesson. An account of recent developments in consultancy is given in Hanko (1985), with particular reference to children with difficulties of behaviour or adjustment.

Although traditional remedial education is undergoing radical reform, major problems remain. Implementation of new approaches is uneven both between and within LEAs. Many schools still have a remedial department or are visited by peripatetic remedial teachers who withdraw children for extra tuition in reading with little time for consultation with school staff. Withdrawal is still the preferred mode of providing extra help in primary schools, as suggested in surveys of current practice (Clunies-Ross and Wimhurst, 1983; Hodgson, Clunies-Ross and Hegarty, 1984; Croll and Moses, 1985).

Nevertheless, an increasing number of schools now see withdrawal as only one of a widening range of options, only to be used where the child's individually assessed needs suggest that this is indeed the most appropriate form of provision. Other alternatives are now being considered. The overall aim of most of these involves the development of a working partnership between the ordinary class teacher and members of teams with particular responsibility for meeting special needs. This partnership can take a variety of forms, depending on particular circumstances and individual preferences. Much depends on the sheer credibility of special needs teachers, their perceived capacity to offer support and advice and, where necessary, direct, practical help.

We can think of the presence of the specialist teacher as being on a continuum of visibility. A 'high-profile' specialist may sit alongside a pupil with special needs, providing direct assistance and support in participating in activities being followed by the rest of the class. A 'low-profile' specialist may join with a colleague in what is in effect a team-teaching situation, perhaps spending a little more time with individuals or groups with special needs. An even lower profile is provided by teachers who may not set foot in the classroom at all but who may spend considerable periods of time in discussion with colleagues on ways in which the curriculum can be made more accessible to all children in the class, including the least able. Such discussions may involve an examination of textbooks and other reading assignments for readability, conceptual difficulty and relevance of content, as well as issues concerned with the presentation of the material, language modes and complexity used to explain what is required, and the use of different approaches to teacher-pupil dialogue.

IMPLICATIONS FOR TEACHER TRAINING

Issues of training are raised by the authors of the three overview works in this series but permeate all the volumes concerned with specific areas of the curriculum or specific areas of special needs.

The scale and complexity of changes taking place in the field of special needs and the necessary transformation of the teacher-training curriculum imply an agenda for teacher training that is nothing less than retraining and supporting every teacher in the country in working with pupils with special needs.

Although teacher training represented one of the three major priorities identified by the Warnock Committee, the resources devoted to this priority have been meagre, despite a strong commitment to training from teachers, LEAs, staff of higher education, HMI and the DES itself. Nevertheless, some positive developments can be noted (for more detailed accounts of developments in teacher education see Sayer and Jones, 1985 and Robson, Sebba, Mittler and Davies, 1988).

Initial training

At the initial training level, we now find an insistence that all teachers in training must be exposed to a compulsory component concerned with meeting special needs in the ordinary school. The Council for the Accreditation of Teacher Education (CATE) and HMI seem set to enforce these criteria; institutions that do not meet them will not be accredited for teacher training.

Although this policy is welcome from a special needs perspective, many questions remain. Where will the staff to teach these courses come from? What happened to the Warnock recommendations for each teacher-training institution to have a small team of staff specifically concerned with this area? Even when a team exists, they can succeed in 'permeating' a special needs element into initial teacher training only to the extent that they influence all their fellow specialist tutors to widen their teaching perspectives to include children with special needs.

Special needs departments in higher education face similar problems to those confronting special needs teams in secondary schools. They need to gain access to and influence the work of the whole institution. They also need to avoid the situation where the very existence of an active special needs department results in colleagues regarding special needs as someone else's responsibility, not theirs.

Despite these problems, the outlook in the long term is favourable. More and more teachers in training are at least receiving an introduction to special needs; are being encouraged to seek out information on special needs policy and practice in the schools in which they are doing their teaching practice, and are being introduced to a variety of approaches to meeting their needs. Teaching materials are being prepared specifically for initial teacher-training students. Teacher trainers have also been greatly encouraged by the obvious interest and commitment of students to children with special needs; optional and elective courses on this subject have always been over-subscribed.

Inservice courses for designated teachers

Since 1983, the government has funded a series of one-term full-time courses in polytechnics and universities to provide intensive training for designated teachers with specific responsibility for pupils with special needs in ordinary schools (see *Meeting Special Needs in Ordinary Schools* by Seamus Hegarty in this series for information on research on evaluation of their effectiveness). These courses are innovative in a number of respects. They bring LEA and higher-education staff together in a productive working partnership. The seconded teacher, headteacher, LEA adviser and higher-education tutor enter into a commitment to train and support the teachers in becoming change agents in their own schools. Students spend two days a week in their own schools initiating and implementing change. All teachers with designated responsibilities for pupils with special needs have the right to be considered for these one-term courses, which are now a national priority area for which central funding is available. However, not all teachers can gain access to these courses as the institutions are geographically very unevenly distributed.

Other inservice courses

The future of inservice education for teachers (INSET) in education in general and special needs in particular is in a state of transition. Since April 1987, the government has abolished the central pooling arrangements which previously funded courses and has replaced these by a system in which LEAs are required to identify their training requirements and to submit these to the DES for funding. LEAs are being asked to negotiate training needs with each school as part of a policy of staff development and appraisal. Special needs is one of nineteen national priority areas that will receive 70 per cent funding from the DES, as is training for further education (FE) staff with special needs responsibilities.

These new arrangements, known as Grant Related Inservice Training (GRIST), will change the face of inservice training for all teachers but time is needed to assess their impact on training opportunities and teacher effectiveness (see Mittler, 1986, for an interim account of the implications of the proposed changes). In the meantime, there is serious concern about the future of secondments for courses longer than one term. Additional staffing will also be needed in higher education to respond to the wider range of demand.

An increasing number of 'teaching packages' have become available for teachers working with pupils with special needs. Some (though not all) of these are well designed and evaluated. Most of them are school-based and can be used by small groups of teachers working under the supervision of a trained tutor.

The best known of these is the Special Needs Action Programme (SNAP) originally developed for Coventry primary schools (Muncey and Ainscow, 1982) but now being adapted for secondary schools. This is based on a form of pyramid training in which co-ordinators from each school are trained to train colleagues in their own school or sometimes in a consortium of local schools. Evaluation by a National Foundation for Educational Research (NFER) research team suggests that SNAP is potentially an effective approach to school-based inservice training, providing that strong management support is guaranteed by the headteacher and by senior LEA staff (see Hegarty, *Meeting Special Needs in Ordinary Schools*, this series, for a brief summary).

Does training work?

Many readers of this series of books are likely to have recent experience of training courses. How many of them led to changes in classroom practice? How often have teachers been frustrated by their inability to introduce and implement change in their schools on returning from a course? How many heads actively support their staff in becoming change agents? How many teachers returning from advanced one-year courses have experienced 'the re-entry phenomenon'? At worst, this is quite simply being ignored: neither the LEA adviser, nor the head nor any one else asks about special interests and skills developed on the course and how these could be most effectively put to good use in the school. Instead, the returning member of staff is put through various re-initiation rituals, ('Enjoyed your holiday?'), or is given responsibilities bearing no relation to interests developed on the course. Not infrequently, colleagues with less experience and fewer qualifications are promoted over their heads during their absence.

At a time of major initiatives in training, it may seem churlish to raise questions about the effectiveness of staff training. It is necessary to do so because training resources are limited and because the morale and motivation of the teaching force depend on satisfaction with what is offered – indeed, on opportunities to negotiate what is available with course providers. Blind faith in training for training's sake soon leads to disillusionment and frustration.

For the last three years, a team of researchers at Manchester University and Huddersfield Polytechnic have been involved in a DES funded project which aimed to assess the impact of a range of inservice courses on teachers working with pupils with special educational needs (see Robson, Sebba, Mittler and Davies, 1988, for a full account and Sebba, 1987, for a briefer interim report). A variety of courses was evaluated; some were held for one evening a week for a term; others were one-week full time; some were award-bearing, others were not. The former included the North-West regional diploma in special needs, the first example of a course developed in total partnership between a university and a polytechnic which allowed students to take modules from either institution and also gave credit recognition to specific Open University and LEA courses. The research also evaluated the effectiveness of an already published and disseminated course on behavioural methods of teaching – the EDY course (Farrell, 1985).

Whether or not the readers of these books are or will be experiencing a training course, or whether their training consists only of the reading of one or more of the books in this series, it may be useful to conclude by highlighting a number of challenges facing teachers and teacher trainers in the coming decades.

1. We are all out of date in relation to the challenges that we face in our work.

2. Training in isolation achieves very little. Training must be seen as part of a wider programme of change and development of the institution as a whole.
3. Each LEA, each school and each agency needs to develop a strategic approach to staff development, involving detailed identification of training and development needs with the staff as a whole and with each individual member of staff.
4. There must be a commitment by management to enable the staff member to try to implement ideas and methods learned on the course.
5. This implies a corresponding commitment by the training institutions to prepare the student to become an agent of change.
6. There is more to training than attending courses. Much can be learned simply by visiting other schools, seeing teachers and other professionals at work in different settings and exchanging ideas and experiences. Many valuable training experiences can be arranged within a single school or agency, or by a group of teachers from different schools meeting regularly to carry out an agreed task.
7. There is now no shortage of books, periodicals, videos and audio-visual aids concerned with the field of special needs. Every school should therefore have a small staff library which can be used as a resource by staff and parents. We hope that the present series of unit texts will make a useful contribution to such a library.

The publishers and I would like to thank the many people – too numerous to mention – who have helped to create this series. In particular we would like to thank the Associate Editors, James Hogg, Peter Pumfrey, Tessa Roberts and Colin Robson, for their active advice and guidance; the Honorary Advisory Board, Neville Bennett, Marion Blythman, George Cooke, John Fish, Ken Jones, Sylvia Phillips, Klaus Wedell and Phillip Williams, for their comments and suggestion; and the teachers, teacher trainers and special needs advisers who took part in our information surveys.

Professor Peter Mittler   University of Manchester
                                                January 1987

REFERENCES

Clunies-Ross, L. and Wimhurst, S. (1983) *The Right Balance: Provision for Slow Learners in Secondary Schools*. Windsor: NFER/Nelson.
Committee of Inquiry (1985) *Education for All*. London: HMSO (The Swann Report).

Croll, P. and Moses, D. (1985) *One in Five: The Assessment and Incidence of Special Educational Needs*. London: Routledge & Kegan Paul.

Farrell, P. (ed.) (1985) *EDY: Its Impact on Staff Training in Mental Handicap*. Manchester: Manchester University Press.

Hanko, G. (1985) *Special Needs in Ordinary Classrooms: An Approach to Teacher Support and Pupil Care in Primary and Secondary Schools*. Oxford: Blackwell.

Hargreaves, D. (1982) *Challenge for the Comprehensive School*. London: Routledge & Kegan Paul.

Hodgson, A., Clunies-Ross, L. and Hegarty, S. (1984) *Learning Together*. Windsor: NFER/Nelson.

Inner London Education Authority (1984) *Improving Secondary Education*. London: ILEA (The Hargreaves Report).

Inner London Education Authority (1985a) *Improving Primary Schools*. London: ILEA (The Thomas Report).

Inner London Education Authority (1985b) *Equal Opportunities for All?* London: ILEA (The Fish Report).

Mittler, P. (1986) The new look in inservice training. *British Journal of Special Education*, **13**, pp. 50–51.

Muncey, J. and Ainscow, M. (1982) Launching SNAP in Coventry. *Special Education: Forward Trends*, **10**, pp. 3–5.

Robson, C., Sebba, J., Mittler, P. and Davies, G. (1988) *Inservice Training and Special Needs: Running Short School-Focused Courses*. Manchester: Manchester University Press.

Sayer, J. and Jones, N. (eds.) (1985) *Teacher Training and Special Educational Needs*. Beckenham: Croom Helm.

Sebba, J. (1987) The development of short, school-focused INSET courses in special educational needs. *Research Papers in Education* (in press).

Topping, K. and Wolfendale, S. (eds) (1985) *Parental Involvement in Children's Reading*. Beckenham: Croom Helm.

Wedge, P. and Prosser, H. (1973) *Born to Fail?* London: National Children's Bureau.

Widlake, P. (1984) *How to Reach the Hard to Teach*. Milton Keynes: Open University Press.

Widlake, P. (1985) *Reducing Educational Disadvantage*. London: Routledge & Kegan Paul.

Introduction

Detailed discussion of the major implications of the Warnock Report and the 1981 Education Act can be found in other volumes in this series and elsewhere. The purpose of this book is more practical. We seek to outline how these changes have already affected those responsible for the teaching of humanities subjects in secondary schools. We will suggest practical ways in which some of the problems that are encountered may be overcome both by teachers of humanities subjects who happen to find children with special educational needs in their classroom, and by those who may have a more general responsibility for the humanities curriculum in the secondary school. In addition we hope that our thoughts will be of interest to heads of special needs departments. Their responsibilities may extend both to curriculum design for children who might remain or join in special classes within the comprehensive school and to the encouragement and support of the heads of other faculties within their schools.

As practising teachers we are only too aware of the pressures which exist upon schools in a time of rapid change and relatively limited resources. We realise that humanities departments, as others, are greatly concerned with the implementation of the GCSE and are engaged upon the writing of coursework assessment proposals and the search for new resources to cope with the demands of what for many will be a new departure. We are also aware that trends towards profiling and the desire of some humanities departments to involve themselves in the preparation of modules of local environmental studies as part of some pre-vocational course all bring their own stresses upon human and material resources. The curriculum debate in the humanities and the publication of HMI documents on the teaching of history and geography have challenged some traditional assumptions and some practice. All these have combined to make the task of the humanities teacher difficult, especially in the ordering of priorities.

Our hope is that in a deluge of new ideas in the humanities, the interests of those with special educational needs will not be washed away. In fact, we shall argue that many of these new trends, especially GCSE and profiling, can be seen as following a model which has its roots in special education, and that the assessment techniques of the new examination and the setting of tight objectives are precisely those which can be of great applicability to those involved with the teaching of children with special educational needs. It may be that the GCSE itself is an inappropriate vehicle for this population in the 14–16 age group. However, teachers who are familiar with the underlying philosophy of the examination will find it an easy step to offer a meaningful curriculum to those for whom the examination was not designed. We shall argue then that the modern trends in secondary education which make so many demands of teachers do not make these demands in different directions. The intellectual philosophy which underpins them is the same.

The first chapter will set out the scope of this book. It will detail our working definitions of humanities and secondary schools, it will explore briefly the notion of special educational needs and will discuss at more length the nature of learning difficulties which some children experience in humanities subjects.

—1—

Definitions and parameters

HUMANITIES

There has been a continuing debate as to what actually constitute the 'humanities' in secondary schools. Some schools are organised with humanities faculties; others are not. In some schools geography teaching will be regarded as lying within the humanities field; in others it will be regarded as more of a scientific discipline. Some schools will have abandoned traditional subject areas in favour of an integrated, combined or inter-disciplinary approach to the whole curricular area which they will follow throughout the age range; others will have maintained the traditional separateness, and the idea of 'humanities' subjects will mean little. The curriculum debate since 1975, stimulated by a plethora of documents from the centre, has demanded that school subjects justify themselves in terms of relevance to the school population and to the wider society. This has led, not only to an increased concentration on curricular matters and on the evaluation of courses, but also to claims for the unique place of particular subjects within the school curriculum. Pertinent to this discussion are HMI documents on curriculum matters, e.g. *The Teaching of Ideas in Geography* (DES, 1978), *Geography 5–16* (DES, 1986), *History Matters* (DES, 1985a) and related work such as *History in the Primary and Secondary Years* (DES, 1985b).

Many schools will be organised on lines which provide for a faculty structure and a whole range of subjects may fall underneath the heading of humanities. Often those subjects which are so placed will be there for a variety of reasons which may be concerned with matters of educational principle, or may be simple responses to the constraints of staffing. This is especially true in a time when many local authorities and schools have had to cope with the problems of falling rolls. The specialist in economics, for example, might be an inexperienced teacher who is therefore placed within the humanities faculty so that a more senior member of staff may oversee professional development. In other schools heads of department in history and geography may be experienced and the organisation of the school has never seen it politic to amalgamate them into one faculty or larger department. A whole range of *ad hoc* arrangements may well have been made to accommodate different subjects into different groupings.

We do not wish to embroil ourselves in the debate as to whether there should be a faculty structure for the humanities subjects or whether they should stand in their traditional compartments within the structure of the school. Equally, we do not wish to lay down guidelines as to what should be taught. While we shall be offering examples of syllabuses and individual lessons, these are selected to demonstrate essential principles and are intended to do nothing more than to demonstrate how particular skills and content can be positively and beneficially presented to children with special educational needs. Indeed it would be folly to prescribe the content of the humanities curriculum since this can be seen as almost infinite. While our own view of appropriate content will be clear in our choice of examples this does not imply that only that content is appropriate. Our task, essentially, is to suggest ways in which schools and teachers can adapt their materials and teaching styles to bring the basic curriculum within the range and comprehension of the child with special educational needs, whatever the individual school has decided that curriculum to be.

For this reason our definition of 'humanities' is arbitrary and wide ranging and is based on the following criterion. Simply, we define a humanities subject for the purposes of this book as one which we would not be surprised to find under the umbrella of a humanities faculty. These include, geography, history, integrated humanities, world studies, social studies/science, economics, sociology, politics, and religious education. Other subjects which might appear in a more comprehensive list are dealt with in other volumes in this series.

SECONDARY SCHOOLS

We hope that our thoughts will be of use to teachers in comprehensive schools and most of our material is aimed at teachers of the 11–16 age group. We hope, however, that teachers in middle schools, where these exist, may also find information of value to them, and that the general principles and instructional techniques will be of use to those working with some students in sixth form colleges.

CHILDREN WITH SPECIAL EDUCATIONAL NEEDS

Our purpose is to provide strategies for teachers who face problems with children who find humanities subjects difficult. We shall avoid the use of labels as far as possible and resist the temptation to enter the debate over definitions in the belief that this is unhelpful and often counter productive. As teachers, we are not interested in whether a child is classified as having learning difficulties which are described as 'mild', 'moderate' or 'severe'. As deputy heads or heads of year we would, of course, find such classifications helpful since they are the jargon terms used by other professionals with whom we have to deal, but as classroom teachers we would be anxious to dismiss them from our thoughts since none of these terms explain to us how we can best encourage success and prevent failure in the children themselves.

To use the terminology of the 1981 Education Act, we are interested in those children who have significantly greater difficulty in learning the skills and concepts of humanities disciplines than the majority of children of their age. The Warnock Report suggested that at some time during their school career 20 per cent of pupils might have a special need (DES, 1978). Of these some would continue to be educated in special schools but the vast majority, 18 per cent of the total school population identified by Warnock, would remain in mainstream schools, and most within fully integrated mainstream classes. Of the remaining 2 per cent it is envisaged that a proportion of them would join mainstream schools in the future although most, because of the nature of their needs as set out in the annual statement, would be taught in special classes. In numerical terms this means that an average mixed-ability lower school class of 30 children would include approximately 5 children with learning difficulties. It would also include another 7 children for whom the GCE/CSE system of examinations at 16+ was not designed. Of course, the 20 per cent are not necessarily the pupils who have the greatest difficulty in learning. It is a changing group and contains pupils whose special needs does not hinder their learning, if, for example, the physical environment is modified. However, our concern is only marginally with this group. Our chief interest is with those who, under a different classification, used to be called 'slow learners'.

We should indicate at this point that to consider these matters solely in numerical terms is misleading. In the first place different schools will vary widely in their numbers of children with learning difficulties. The Geographical Association's survey (1982), for example, discovered that teachers' estimates of the proportion of 11-year-olds considered to be 'less able' varied widely from school to school in its sample, from 7 per cent or 8 per cent in one school to 40–50 per cent in another. This is partly because of the nature of the intake of different schools and partly because of the ways in which schools organise themselves and the level of their expectations. For example, one of us has recently visited a school which was seeking strategies to assist children who had learning difficulties in reading. She discovered that in this school a number of children were having significantly greater difficulty in English than others in the same year group. Investigation revealed that this school, because of the nature of its intake over the years, had developed a level of expectation of its pupils considerably higher than most and that the level of difficulty of the reading books covered in the first year was that which most schools would not have introduced until the start of the third year. This particular school had identified its population of children with learning difficulties but many of these same children would not have been identified as being in this category had they gone to a different school.

Secondly, the numbers of children with learning difficulties within each class will vary. It is unlikely that there would be an even distribution of these children across all classes even in a school which pursued a firm policy of mixed-ability grouping throughout the age range. Even if these children were evenly distributed at the start of a school year the situation would soon change if particular weaknesses of individuals were removed or if others became apparent. More importantly, the number is dependent not only on changes within the children themselves, but also on the content of the lessons. Some children who are, apparently, slow in the learning of a particular point in a history lesson may not be slow to learn the main point of next week's lesson. Children will find certain aspects of courses more difficult than others. For example, Cowie (1979) has indicated that some children will have difficulty in history lessons since their understanding of tense is limited and that this will present problems in coping with historical time. However, she goes on to point out that this is an aspect of historical study in which a large number of children will experience difficulty: 'Most pupils have language difficulties in history' and 'more successful pupils disguise their problems by being able to manipulate other people's language without necessarily understanding fully what they are saying or writing' (p. 10). In other words it is an area of the humanities curriculum that produces learning difficulties for many children, including those for whom other areas in the humanities present no problems. In terms of courses and individual lessons the level of learning difficulty is content dependent. To view the numbers of children with learning difficulties within the school or the class as static is to miss the point both of the 1981 legislation and of the nature of learning difficulties.

Nevertheless, for the sole purpose of establishing parameters, and to indicate the scale of the problem, it is with this group of, approximately, 18 per cent of the school population that we are primarily concerned: those children who are fully integrated into mainstream classes. We also hope that our ideas might be of use to those whose responsibility it is to design a curriculum for children within special classes, where these exist. The evidence is that while, philosophically, there is a movement away from removing children from ordinary classes and placing them in special classes (see Chapter 2), nevertheless many schools continue to operate this type of system. So, in addition to providing techniques for humanities teachers who may be unsure of how best to proceed in their work with children who have learning difficulties, we would hope to be able to present strategies that would be useful to non-specialists interested in doing some humanities work.

While we have some pages concerned with particular forms of special needs, including a number of thoughts on fieldwork for non-ambulant children and problems that teachers may have with examination boards in terms of designing papers for partially sighted children, most of this work is concerned with children with learning difficulties, since there are strong arguments to suggest that it is this group which is most likely to be forgotten.

Our own experience, for example, is of working in a situation which is the integrated resource school for one LEA for secondary school age children with physical handicaps. While we would not claim that the integration process has been without difficulty, nevertheless the statementing procedure for special educational needs as detailed in the 1981 Act, though lengthy, has the beneficial effect of concentrating minds upon the precise needs of the individual child. Meeting the needs, for example, of a child who is partially sighted becomes a matter of discovering what aids are available and requesting these pieces of hardware in the annual review so that enlarging scanners, portable typewriters and more powerful photocopiers, etc. become available. Professional minds are focused by the annual review: a procedure exists for meeting special needs. Previously, this child would have been one whose educational needs would have been met in a special school. Consequently, it is clear to all in the mainstream school that the needs of this pupil are 'special' and all attempts are made to provide a framework in which the mainstream curriculum can be made accessible to that pupil.

However, for the remainder of children with special educational needs, the 18 per cent, the position is much less clear. Most of these children would, by definition under the previous arrangements, have been educated in ordinary schools, and consequently main-stream teachers are used to the presence of these children in their schools. These are the children who find 'success' in terms of traditional academic achievement in school difficult to achieve, those for whom the CSE was not designed and those who were not envisaged by the Secretary of State in 1985 to be capable of attaining a foundation Grade in GCSE examinations. No statementing procedure exists for them. (While it would theoretically be possible to initiate this procedure in practice constraints of time are so great that this would be extremely rare.) It is possible, that the interests of these children are pushed aside and most efforts made with those who are the subject of statements. It is with this large group that we are primarily concerned.

Learning difficulties in the humanities

In practical terms the sorts of difficulty exhibited by children in humanities subjects are well known to teachers and well documented. General agreement exists as to the specific problems which children and therefore teachers are likely to face. We are not concerned (see Chapter 2) with the aetiology of learning difficulties and we do not think it helpful to attempt to build up a 'profile' of the child with learning difficulties in humanities subjects. What follows is a list of some of those aspects of humanities learning which some children find difficult and of some behaviours exhibited by them. It is useful to know the sorts of difficulties which are faced so that teachers can better address them.

Some of these difficulties may be seen in other areas of the school curriculum and some are specific to humanities lessons. Certain apparently 'general difficulties' or special needs that particular children have in learning can have more or less pronounced effect in humanities lessons. For example, a child who is confined to a wheelchair should have no more difficulty in a geography or a history classroom than others, provided that there is access to the room and to the resources within it. It is possible that being wheelchair bound might have entailed a lack of early experiential learning that led to later learning difficulties. The same child, however, presents much greater problems in the sports hall. Non-ambulance will, in most instances, make no difference to the child in humanities lessons whereas a modified curriculum might be appropriate in PE. So it is with other difficulties. It may be of little interest for the science teacher to know that a child has difficulty in orienting a map of the world. For the geography teacher, however, such a difficulty may be crucial and may require thought, the preparation of special materials and a modified teaching style from that normally used.

A general observation made about children with learning difficulties concerns their motivation. While we would accept the dictum that 'less able does not necessarily mean less interested'

(Higginbottom and Renwick, 1983), nevertheless many commentators have indicated that motivation is a major problem in history and geography lessons both in this country and the USA (e.g. Corney and Rawling, 1985; Sharp, 1981). This is clearly a difficulty which some children are likely to have across the curriculum, not one which applies only in humanities subjects. However, Wilson's researches (1982) are illuminating in this respect. Although the scale of the research was small, he found that low achievers exhibited poor motivation in their study of history, specifically. They questioned its relevance and expressed dissatisfaction with the teaching methods employed and generally were much more critical of their history lessons than with other curricular areas, including other literary subjects. A fuller discussion of the reasons for poor motivation together with curricular and pedagogic implications can be found in Chapter 2.

Burnison (1982) noted that other aspects of general learning which are likely to have implications for the teaching of history are:

- poor attainment in reading;
- lack of facility in writing;
- poor memory;
- short span of attention;
- limited powers of discussion – although there is some dispute about this (see Wilson, 1985; Hodgkinson and Long, 1981);
- difficulties with concept development.

These suggestions are mirrored by geographers:

- poor concentration;
- difficulty in the handling of abstractions;
- poor language, reading and spelling and an inability to use 'standard' material;
- difficulty in achieving satisfaction and enjoyment;
- apprehension about number work;
- lack of logical sequencing and a failure to understand simple causation.

The Geographical Association's survey (1982) indicated that reading, writing and number work were the basic skills most frequently mentioned by teachers, together with limited concentration spans; difficulties experienced with generalisation and abstract ideas, memorising information and the appreciation of alternative viewpoints. As one teacher in Bines's research put it:

Pupils really need to absorb information, remember it, then apply it in another situation, which they find very difficult. The best can, the average have difficulty remembering what the facts were in the first place, let alone applying it to another situation and this is where the kids with problems really fall down.

(1986, p. 63)

In terms of subject specific difficulties which children experience, Cowie suggests that in history children find it difficult to 'see links, find relationships, make contrasts, generalisations or discriminate. ... Often they seem to lack the qualities which are essential for the historian – imagination, curiosity and long-distance memory'. Clearly this is extremely important. While the study of history is not 'linear' in the sense that the study of a foreign language is, i.e. success in the subject does not rely entirely on having grasped the essential principles taught in previous lessons, nevertheless much of the historian's work is concerned with the drawing of parallels. An apparent inability to hold information and ideas in the head from one lesson to the next places the child with difficulties at a severe disadvantage: it is much easier to understand the internal history of Nazi Germany if the essential aspects of Mussolini's regime in Italy, which were studied a fortnight ago, can be remembered. Similarly, children are more likely to reach a conceptual understanding of the causes of the plight of nineteenth-century handloom weavers if they can remember the work they had already done on working conditions in the early Industrial Revolution; if they have no recollection of earlier lessons the task becomes more difficult.

Cowie also indicates that children with learning difficulties cannot cope adequately with the ways in which historical material is presented in terms of the density of print, type or writing and the lack of visual stimulus. While school-produced material can easily overcome these problems (see Chapter 4), it is nevertheless true that current aims in the teaching of history do make considerable demands on these children in terms of the handling of evidence. Few teachers of history would disagree with the GCSE National Criteria which state that a history course should give children the opportunity:

> To show the skills necessary to study a wide variety of historical evidence which should include both primary and secondary written sources, statistical and visual material, artefacts, textbooks and orally transmitted information.
>
> (National Criteria for History, para 3.4)

The study of a wide variety of evidence may itself involve great problems for children with learning difficulties. This is true both in terms of the presentation of the evidence and in terms of the content of the evidence. It is especially true since, added to forms of historical evidence which history teachers have traditionally used, they now have to add data of a mathematical nature – pie charts, histograms, percentages – all of which, arguably, are the effective ways to give meaning to such evidence as census returns. Also, the historian needs to embrace the problems presented by visual stimuli and maps. While the inclusion of visual material may brighten up history lessons and ease the problem of motivation for children with learning difficulties, actually to study visual stimuli of an historical nature addressing the problems of bias, for example, is not easy and requires special skills of its own. The same is true with watching the many videos which have been prepared for use in history lessons. The teacher needs to be aware of what is going on inside the head of the recipient of these visual signals, and to act as an interpreter of them if children with learning difficulties are not to find visual material as puzzling as the written word. Equally, the use of the historical cartoon in classrooms, which is becoming increasingly popular, is a minefield for the unwary. To see the point and the subtlety of a political cartoon is a task which troubles many of the highest achievers, and teachers need to be aware that low achievers require specialised help if they are to gain much from studying them.

In the area of mapwork, historians and geographers face similar problems, but clearly they are greater for the geographers. Commentators see graphicacy – the communication of spatial information that cannot be conveyed adequately by verbal or numerical means – as one of the central skills of geography and that which gives children with learning difficulties many problems. There is a wealth of literature on this. Indeed the report on *Teaching Geography to Less Able 11–14 Year Olds* suggests that of all geographical skills this was the one which gave some children most difficulty (Corney and Rawling, 1985).

> Many teachers referred at length to difficulties associated with using OS maps. Map skills evoked more comment in this respect than any other [geographical] skill. Understanding scale was identified as the most common area of difficulty. One teacher suggested that 1:50.000 was too small a scale for less able pupils to work with; 1:1.250 or larger would be more appropriate. Other difficulties were related to understanding the map as a two dimensional representation of three dimensional reality, to interpreting contours and sections and to using grid references and symbols.
>
> (p. 8)

Booth (1980) suggests that since maps and models are abstractions, children who require information to be presented in a more concrete form will find them extremely difficult. As Boardman (1984) has demonstrated, the understanding of maps and carto-graphic communication is a complex learning problem which many children find difficult. Catling (1985) suggests that the understand-ing of maps develops gradually and practically and that for many pupils 'their understanding of map skills and concepts is far from complete at the age of 16 years'. McNamara (1982) argues that 'mapwork is not just difficult, but may well be impossible'. He identifies the essence of the learning problem:

> In presenting a child [with learning difficulties] with a map we may be asking ... [them] to take a two dimensional perception, transfer it cognitively into a three dimensional conception, make inferences from this conception and transfer them back into perception. Put this way, it becomes a wonder that any pupils can do it, let alone a slow learning child in the first year of a secondary school.
>
> (p. 30)

An area, largely neglected in the literature, but one which seems to us to be of paramount importance, is that concerning background knowledge. A study completed at the Aberdeen College of Education found that inadequate background knowledge was often the reason for failure. With the possible exception of some English courses there is no collection of disciplines on the secondary school curriculum, apart from those loosely grouped under the humanities umbrella, for which 'general knowledge' is so important. For high achievers, especially those with supportive parents, humanities subjects are frequently an opportunity to demonstrate skills and knowledge which have been gained outside school.

All manner of skills pertinent to the understanding of concepts in the humanities are acquired outside school. At a simple level the encouragement which children receive from parents and others to engage in activities outside school may affect their performance within it. Arguably, map skills, for example, can be acquired more easily outside school than within it. Boy Scouts or those engaged on a Duke of Edinburgh's Award scheme may have learned advanced map skills, such as re-sections, and be very well aware of the difference in degrees between magnetic north and grid north. We know of a girl whose father competes in two-day Mountain Marathons twice a year. These involve both running and orienteer-ing, scoring points for various checkpoints visited. He spends the two weeks prior to each event making three dimensional balsa wood models of what he believes will be the competitive area, tracing the contours on the OS map, cutting round them and building a 3D picture of the area on his balsa model, in the hope that this visual representation will give him an advantage over other competitors. He has enlisted the help of his daughter in this biannual enterprise. Her performance in geography demonstrates this frequent reinforcement of essential mapping concepts.

Parents who travel with their children or take them on frequent visits, *provided that they present them with an interpretation and explanation of the places they visit and the things which they see,* giving them what Feuerstein refers to as a 'mediated learning experience' (1980), do much of the humanities teachers' job for them. In a rare example, a child of secondary school age who has visited a city in a developing country and who has been personally exposed to the problems of that city in terms of shanty towns, a creaking transport system and an unstable currency is likely to know as much about the topic as the teacher. Children who have seen the memorial on the Thiepval Ridge on the Somme battlefield, who have walked along the zig-zagged front line trenches and who have seen No Man's Land or who have peered through the window of the Ossuary at Verdun are likely to possess a much deeper understanding of the realities of First World War combat, in terms of the wastage of life and the reasons for it, than could ever be achieved in a classroom.

Closer to home, teachers of history will be familiar with the children who have been to the Viking Museum at York or to Housesteads Fort and who can therefore delight in displaying their knowledge and understanding of Viking and Roman culture. Similarly, children who travel in the cabs of their fathers' trucks in holiday time find classroom explanations of the motorway system of Britain and the relationship between the movement of goods and the construction of these roads much more easy to understand. Equally, children who have experienced racism, or problems connected with the religious beliefs of their family, are likely to be able to understand empathetically the plight of the Jews in Nazi Germany, possibly better than their teachers if they have never directly experienced racial or religious hostility. In all these cases the personal experience of these children is a much greater resource for their learning than anything which the teacher can provide in the classroom.

So much of humanities learning concerns things which are far away in space or time. The science teacher or the maths teacher does not always have this problem. The toad in the biology laboratory, although in captivity, behaves much as other toads do. The pulse rate of a child's classmate will increase with exercise and gradually decrease when it is over, as will pulse rates all over the world. A right-angled triangle is the same everywhere, the same for 4B's lesson as it was for Pythagoras. Rio de Janeiro or Queen Elizabeth I, on the other hand, can only be brought into the classroom artificially. Humanities teachers have to import the world into their classrooms and those children who have experienced that world through their life outside school are placed at an advantage. Correspondingly those who have not are, in relative terms, impoverished.

This is also true even in terms of general political, economic and sociological understanding. What happens at home can have a profound impact on the confidence and success of a child in humanities subjects. The daily newspaper read at home or the TV programmes watched there reaffirm classroom knowledge in many curricular areas. In humanities their influence may be enormous. Teachers will be aware of the difficulties which arise in schools when lessons on current affairs are planned. Many children have little idea about recent events in a local or national sense and immediately they are placed at a disadvantage relative to other children. In terms of humanities subjects then, the issue of background knowledge is vital.

> The teacher has to consider whether the symbols on an Ordnance Survey map mean very much to 11 year old children. If they have not experienced a train journey, for example, the difference between an ordinary station and a principal station may not be apparent to them. Children who have never walked along a canal towpath may not always appreciate the difference between a canal and a river. For children who have never visited the sea, such symbols as those depicting cliffs, flat rocks, sand and shingle probably have little meaning for them.
>
> (Boardman, 1986, p. 28)

It has been demonstrated that children with learning difficulties are less likely to belong to a library, a church or an organised group; they travel away from their local area less, they visit art galleries, exhibitions, museums, theatres less frequently than do higher achievers (Brennan, 1974). Teachers, especially those trained in the humanities, should question the cause and effect of this situation. Is it that children visit these places and belong to these organisations less frequently than others because they have learning difficulties, or rather is it that they have learning difficulties because they do not visit them or belong to them? We would tend towards the latter interpretation and claim that some apparent problems which children have in humanities lessons which are termed learning difficulties are not, strictly, learning difficulties at all. We would suggest that they are manifestations of nothing more than a lack of background knowledge or skills – what we shall be referring to later as pre-skills, or prerequisite knowledge (see Chapter 4).

Children are likely to find the relevance of lessons which take a starting point completely outside their experience difficult to appreciate. Understanding will not come easily.

> For the slow learners the approach to a topic such as work in cotton mills at the time of the Industrial Revolution had to be carefully planned to include explanations of the source and nature of raw materials and of the spinning and weaving processes – otherwise the lessons were meaningless. Again a worksheet on the production of iron in the eighteenth century was not very helpful to a third-year class of girls in a London comprehensive school as they did not know what charcoal was, still less how it was made or used.
>
> (Cowie, 1979, p. 11)

In humanities subjects it is possible that children may be labelled as having learning difficulties even though, intellectually, there may be nothing different about them when compared with higher achievers. It is the nature of the humanities subjects that a lack of background knowledge can penalise some children to a greater extent than it does elsewhere in the school curriculum. There is a much greater danger in humanities lessons, therefore, that teachers can believe their pupils unable to learn, whereas the reality is that they are nothing more than ignorant. This whole area is explored more fully in Chapter 2.

REFERENCES

Bines, H. (1986) *Redefining Remedial Education*. London: Croom Helm.

Boardman, D. (1984) *New Directions in Geographical Education*. London: The Falmer Press.

Boardman, D. (1986) 'Map reading skills'. In Boardman, D. (ed.) *Handbook for Geography Teachers*. Sheffield: Geographical Association.

Booth, M. (1980) Teaching geography to lower ability children. *Teaching Geography* 5 (3), pp. 99–104.

Brennan, W. K. (1974) *Shaping the Education of Slow Learners*. London: Routledge.

Burnison, W. (1982) 'Slow learning children and their problems'. In McIver, V. (ed.) *Teaching History to Slow Learning Children in Secondary Schools*. Belfast: Learning Resources Unit.

Catling, S. J. (1985) 'Mapwork'. In Corney, G. and Rawling, E. (eds) *Teaching Slow Learners through Geography*. Sheffield: Geographical Association.

Corney, G. and Rawling, E. (eds) (1985) *Teaching Slow Learners through Geography*. Sheffield: Geographical Association.

Cowie, E. (1979) *History and the Slow Learning Child: a Practical Approach*.

Teaching of History Series No. 41. London: The Chaucer Press.

DES (1978) *The Teaching of Ideas in Geography*. DES HMI Series: Matters for Discussion 5. London: HMSO.

DES (1985a) *History Matters*. London: HMSO.

DES (1985b) *History in the Primary and Secondary Years – An HMI View*. London: HMSO.

DES (1985c) *General Certificate of Secondary Education – The National Criteria for History*. London: HMSO.

Feuerstein, R. (1980) *Instrumental Enrichment*. Baltimore: The University Press.

Geographical Association (1982) *Teaching Geography to Less Able 11–14 Year Olds: Report of a Survey carried out by the working group on new techniques and methods in teaching Geography*. Sheffield: Geographical Association.

Higginbottom, T. and Renwick, M. (1983) Springboards for Change. *Times Educational Supplement*. December 2.

Hodgkinson, K. and Long, M. (1981) The assassination of John F. Kennedy. *Teaching History* **29**, pp. 3–7.

McNamara, D. (1982) 'Developing mapping skills'. In Boardman, D. (ed.) *Geography with Slow Learners*. Sheffield: Geographical Association.

Sharp, L. S. (1981) Project Heroes: A humanities curriculum for the learning disabled. *Academic Therapy* **16** (5).

Wilson, M. D. (1982) The history curriculum for slow learners. *Teaching History* **32**, pp. 11–13.

Wilson, M. D. (1985) *History for Children with Learning Difficulties*. London: Hodder and Stoughton.

—2———————————————————

Problems and possibilities

THE SETTING

It is our view that children with learning difficulties in the humanities have long been neglected in secondary schools. In relative terms, their needs have not been sufficiently considered compared with those of high achievers. The status of teachers who work with children who have learning difficulties, whether they be specialists in this area, or subject teachers, has not been high, although much lip-service to the efforts of these teachers has been paid. Frequently, subject teachers working in the humanities have been tempted to shed the responsibility for these children to others within or outside the school, and, in some cases, to doubt the relevance and importance of their subjects for children who find them difficult. This chapter will explore the reasons for these trends; it will indicate ways in which the legacy of Warnock and changes in the philosophy of remedial education place much greater responsibilities on subject teachers for the education of children with learning difficulties, particularly in the humanities.

While the function of secondary schooling has been debated endlessly in England and Wales, the recent moves towards the publication of examination results in many LEAs has left no doubt in the minds of schools and wider society that, whatever else they exist for, one important function of schools is the production of 'good' examination results at 16+. This development has tended to reinforce the traditional, tacit view of what constitutes a 'good' school and secondary teachers generally are well aware of the importance of examination results to the reputation of their school in the wider community. Much of the job of teaching is concerned with the organisation of resources, both material and personnel, and the setting of priorities. It would be fanciful to suggest that teachers, generally, have neglected their examination classes along with those children lower down the school who, in their perception, will form the examination classes of years to come, in favour of those who are perceived to have little chance of academic success. Traditionally, working with children with learning difficulties within the humanities department has received relatively low priority.

Knowledge of one's subject in humanities teaching and the ability to convey this with measurable success to examination classes has been one of the keys to promotion, at least to the level of head of department. It would be surprising if this were not the case since the evidence suggests that, generally, those who work with children with learning difficulties are over-represented on the basic salary scale. Frequently the pages of the educational press reveal the existence of posts in which 'an opportunity to teach to 'A' level is available to a well qualified candidate'. Rarely is 'an opportunity to teach geography to children with learning difficulties' available to a well qualified candidate. While we would not wish to suggest that the community of secondary school teachers doubts the importance of work with children with learning difficulties, nevertheless it is work which has received a low priority. High status in secondary schools is likely to be vested in those who are successful 'subject' teachers, not in those whose concerns are with the pedagogic aspects of teaching. It seems clear that the hope, in 1975, of the President of the National Association for Remedial Education that 'the ability to teach less able children must be seen as a skill equal to that of the good subject teacher' has yet to be realised (Widlake, 1975, p. 107).

Low status, among other factors, has led to poor performance. The last twenty years have seen a number of reports from the DES which have pointed to the inadequacies of work with children with learning difficulties. While none of these reports has concentrated on humanities teaching specifically, it is safe to assume that this area of the curriculum suffers from the same deficiencies as others. The Plowden Report, for example, recognised the need for all teachers to be better prepared for work with children who have learning difficulties, while the *Survey of Slow Learners in Secondary Schools* pointed out that 'the needs of the slowest pupils seem to have received less than their share of consideration'. Yet, in the training of teachers, Gulliford has detected a lack of commitment towards providing entrants into the profession with the skills they need to cope with the full ability range (1983). Gains (1980) has questioned the validity of the evidence on which the DES survey was based. This indicated that two-thirds of probationary teachers considered that they had been adequately prepared for teaching less able children (Gains, 1980).

The ways in which secondary schools have been organised have, perhaps paradoxically, contributed to this neglect. The creation and operation of remedial departments has led to insecurity and a confusion of responsibility. It has allowed some humanities teachers to believe that to spend vast amounts of time in creating additional resources and teaching strategies to make the educational experience of children with learning difficulties more fulfilling is neither appreciated nor their responsibility. The existence of remedial departments may have confirmed in the minds of humanities teachers that, perhaps, these children with learning difficulties have not really been their concern. This may have been especially true in the humanities since an individual teacher would, in a traditional framework of individual subject departments, rarely have seen a class more than once, or at the most twice a week, especially in the lower school. The question of 'where even to begin?' may have appeared daunting, and better left to the 'experts' in the remedial department. The existence of remedial departments effectively 'deskilled' subject teachers who found themselves teaching groups which included children with learning difficulties.

An analogous situation occurred in many schools at the time of comprehensive reorganisation. Partly to establish more rigorous procedures for 'guidance' within the school, and partly to accommodate teachers from widely differing backgrounds within the same organisational structure, 'academic' matters were frequently separated from those which were viewed as 'pastoral'. Different structures – heads of department with their subject teachers, heads of year with their form tutors, each responsible to a different deputy head – were created in each secondary school and problems of communication and responsibility occurred. In some cases the effect was to reinforce the view of subject teachers that their job was to teach their subject rather than the children. There was a temptation for them to refer children who were poorly behaved to the head of year rather than to make any attempt to discover what the causes of poor behaviour were, themselves. Similarly, Lloyd-Smith (1979) has argued that the existence of a unit for disruptive pupils can have the effect of reducing individual teachers' commitment to seeking the causes of disruption themselves and trying to solve those problems. As Galloway (1985) has written: 'when schools create specialists to deal with children with problems, it becomes easier for class and subject teachers to transfer responsibility from themselves on to the specialists' (p. 113).

Through the existence of remedial departments in schools, it became possible for a similar shedding of responsibility to occur. Perhaps the Board of Education in 1937 was wise before the event when, writing in *The Education of Backward Children* of the dangers of setting up what would today be called a peripatetic service for children with special educational needs, it warned that: 'the creation of a new class of specialist peripatetic teachers ... would be as likely to hinder as to help the spread of knowledge and skill in handling backward children, because of the temptation which would beset the teachers in the schools to depend on such outside help than rather upon their own resources'. (p. 16)

If we were to substitute 'remedial department' for 'specialist peripatetic teachers' in this quotation we see the essence of the problem. Traditionally, in many schools, children with learning difficulties have been separated out from the mainstream. Initially this was achieved by streaming or by the creation of special classes; later and sometimes in addition, remedial withdrawal was instigated which had the same effect. In both cases a group of specialist teachers was set aside to deal with them. As such, these children have frequently been seen not as the responsibility of the individual humanities teacher while they are in his or her class, as other children are, but instead as the responsibility of the remedial department. Here they received a limited diet which consisted, very largely, of basic skills in which the essential skills and concepts of humanities subjects were rarely approached. The traditional view was that if children did not possess 'basic skills' then the function of the school was to ensure that these were acquired first and before any others. Humanities teachers, perhaps, followed this line believing, for example, that an inability to follow the textbook meant that the children should have their reading improved before history or geography was attempted.

It is easy to comprehend how responsibility, not for the teaching, but for the learning of these children could be shed, and how for many of them their work in humanities lessons was seen as tedious, repetitive, without reason and pointless. In terms of educational theory it seemed clear that little else could be done. Children were offered the traditional diet presented in traditional ways and if they couldn't or didn't eat, they starved, or at least were placed on severely reduced rations.

The approach which traditionally was adopted towards this population has been described as the 'pathological' or 'medical model' (Ainscow and Tweddle, 1977). This dictated that if children did not respond to the curriculum that was offered then there was something wrong with them, that they were 'abnormal', 'pathological' or 'sick' and that, therefore, they should be referred to the remedial department for remediation. If this did not work then there were special schools which were especially designed and equipped for these children. Because of the 'ideology of pathology' it was possible for the 'subject' teachers almost to wash their hands of this part of the school population and to concentrate on those children who were, eventually, to succeed in CSE and 'O' level. As Golby and Gulliver wrote:

> Participation in a subject such as history requires a certain level of literacy, a level determined by the subject itself and the media

through which it is taught. Neither content nor media are open to change. Those pupils who cannot meet this criterion are deemed in need of special help, and the improvement of their condition is to be achieved by remedial techniques which are not part of the normal teacher's function.

(1979, p. 139)

Similarly a geographer has written:

Teachers are often unsure of their ground with these pupils and may, themselves, question the value of the subject to them. Out of sight out of mind in the remedial department ... is preferable to having to do something with them.

(Ciesla, 1979, p. 64)

Closely related to the 'medical' model are techniques of psychological measurement which have been applied with respect to children who have learning difficulties. The measurement of IQ as a predictor of educational performance has been widely used, and arguably has led subject teachers in the humanities to believe that little of value could be done with children who did not perform well in this test. In other curricular areas, English and maths, for example, teachers could see clearly their responsibility for 'basic skills' teaching, since this is part of the business of their trade. Their task was to increase the skills which could be competently demonstrated by this group. Without the basic skills children were unable to reach higher levels in those disciplines. Humanities teachers were tempted to take a different view. They tended to believe that a low IQ meant that children with learning difficulties were unlikely to reach that stage of development known in Piagetian terms as 'formal operational'. They therefore believed that these children were not at that developmental level which was necessary for the comprehension of what history, geography and allied disciplines are really all about. As one geographer suggested, 'slow learners never get past Piaget's concrete operations stage. This tends to mean that they will have difficulty in handling abstract things which are outside their own direct experience' (Booth, 1980, p. 63).

If humanities teachers shared this view, they were in danger of adopting one of three main strategies in their teaching of children with learning difficulties. In the first place some adopted survival tactics which involved doing anything merely to 'keep them quiet'. Secondly some teachers presented material which was largely inappropriate, unmatched to the child's level of competence in humanities. Finally, some abandoned most thoughts of meaningful humanities learning and tailored lessons to the practice of basic skills under the guise of content with a geographical or historical flavour. In the first two cases, levels of failure and frustration increased and in the second little of what humanities in schools has to offer children was presented.

Also, it should be stated that failure has been an integral and necessary part of the system of schooling in England and Wales. Norm-referencing is used in humanities departments and in schools generally. By this method, the progress of children is measured by comparison with what other children do or have done rather than by how well they have reached predetermined curricular objectives. This method of assessment has made it possible for teachers to be content if, for example, 50 per cent of the pupils in a test get 50 per cent of the marks. It has therefore seemed 'natural' for some children to fail. It has become part of the established orthodoxy. Indeed, tests which succeed in placing children on a continuum from 0–100 per cent are praised as being 'good discriminators'. This, however, is the language of chief examiners and not of teachers. In fact some teachers clearly have difficulty in comprehending the reason for examinations and tests. 'Detailed discussion with teachers tended to elicit more comment on the format and content of examination and tests, rather than on the reasons for their use, or on action taken in response to results.' (Geographical Association, 1982, p. 13.) However, it is clear that the idea of success for some clearly legitimised failure for others. More than that, the effect on the motivation of children, as well as teachers, was marked. As the Chairman of the Secondary Examinations Council pointed out:

> We cannot believe that it can be in any way educationally desirable that a pupil of average ability should for the purpose of obtaining a school-leaving certificate be required to attempt an examination paper on which he [sic] is able to obtain only one-third of the possible marks. Such a requirement, far from developing confidence, can only lead to feelings of inadequacy and failure.
>
> (Cockcroft Report, 1982, para 444.)

Clearly, the experience of failure in tests whose main, if not only, purpose was to discover how closely individual performance corresponded to the norm had considerable effect on the self esteem of the children who were failing. This was especially true in those schools that, formally, or through the hidden curriculum, placed a high value on test scores. Some children perceived themselves as outside the community of the school, excluded from examination sets from the age of 14 and, possibly, from the applause of school assemblies which greeted the success of others. School existed for those who succeeded and not for them. Alienation and frustration followed naturally from such impressions.

Behaviour problems frequently accompanied these feelings and teachers found such children almost impossible to motivate. This was especially true in humanities subjects with the prevailing view amongst children that these were not really 'needed' for life outside school. In some children there was a tacit or explicit acknowledgement that the school was correct in its assessment, and therefore the task of the individual teacher was extremely difficult. As Blank (1973) has pointed out, even at the pre-school age some children are heard to say 'I can't, I'm stupid,' and 'I don't know how to do things'. By the fourth or fifth year of secondary school such attitudes can be very entrenched, if they have been confirmed by years of apparent failure to do as well as others in tests and exams which teachers, with the best intentions, have set. As one secondary school geography teacher wrote 'many years of failure at school can mean that a secondary school pupil is unwilling to attempt most tasks because he or she is in the doldrums of despair' (Folland, 1982, p. 39).

In some cases children's self esteem was at odds with the low status which school accorded them and this had profound implications. These children often adopted a defensive stance, unwilling to try to succeed for fear of failure. They simply failed to cope with the demands the school made on them, preferring to subvert and to co-operate as little as possible thus withdrawing from the possibility of failure. The difference between 'coping' and 'defending' it has been suggested is like that between 'playing tennis on the one hand and fighting like fury to stay off the tennis court altogether, on the other' (Bruner, 1966). All teachers of children who have 'defended' in this way will be familiar with those who have seemed to delight, in addition, in breaking the racquets of other players.

It is perhaps for these reasons that there has been a re-examination of the concept of achievement in secondary schools. There has been a widening of appreciation of the pupil behaviours that can be termed achievement. *Improving Secondary Schools* (ILEA, 1984) identified four aspects. There was a recognition of the traditional forms of achievement, the ability to express oneself in the written form, to show mastery of a body of knowledge and to apply that knowledge. In addition the report recognised that there are other aspects of achievement which cannot be tested in the same way, but nevertheless are positive aspects of a student's life in school. Among these were included personal and social skills, being able to work co-operatively and the ability to display initiative and self reliance. Additionally, students can be given credit for demonstrating that they are well motivated, that they can persevere and that they possess the 'willingness to accept failure without destructive consequences' (p. 2).

Many of these aspects of achievement are currently recognised in the development of recording the progress of students by use of profiling. Originally a technique employed by various pre-vocational courses in schools, such as the City and Guilds 365 and CPVE, there has been an extension of profiling into other areas of the school curriculum. It is usual in assessment processes which involve profiles to record aspects of achievement which traditional examination are incapable of testing.

In summary, however, the prevalence of psychometrics in schools led to the danger that teachers of humanities subjects would abandon their responsibilities for the skills and techniques unique to those disciplines. Some believed that children with learning difficulties were unable to cope with these accomplishments. Others considered that they would be better off in pursuing basic skills work to the exclusion of everything else. The cause of this was the belief that IQ demonstrated that some children were unable to acquire those skills necessary for success in their disciplines. Norm-referenced testing carried out regularly throughout the school confirmed this view. The result was the impoverishment of the curriculum followed by these children. Arguably, this had already occurred in schools before IQ testing was widely adopted. The test merely gave the practice 'scientific' validation.

One of the authors remembers a school visit, in the early 1970s, as part of his PGCE studies where he was taken to see a third year secondary class engaged in their history lesson. The task, for the hour, was for each child to colour, in silence, and largely it seemed in purple, a reproduced outline of a medieval street scene. The undying memory is of the teacher's justification of this activity, which was simply to point out that 'there's not much else you can do because these are the remedials'.

THE CHANGING SCENE

The situation in secondary schools is changing. The philosophical assumptions underpinning the education of children with learning difficulties are slowly placing much more of the emphasis in schools not on the remedial specialist nor on the educational psychologist but on the mainstream subject teacher. This position has arisen through the combination of two related strains of thought. Firstly there has been a fresh look at the whole issue of educational need which culminated in the Warnock Report and the 1981 Education Act. Secondly there has been a marked shift of emphasis in the perceptions of remedial education in recent years. Coincidentally, perhaps, the two have come together to create a powerful force for change that is likely to have important implications for the organisation of humanities departments and the work done within them. It is not simply a matter of exchanging one set of labelling jargon for another. In a real sense, theory and practice of the education of children with learning difficulties is in the process of redefinition.

In the first instance a proportion of those in what has been referred to as 'the community of Remedial Education' have envisaged a much wider role for the 'remedial' or 'special needs' teacher than was formerly recognised. They no longer see the sole function of these teachers as being concerned with individual withdrawal of children and support for their learning, a rôle which has been referred to as an 'ambulance service'. This aspect of remedial education has had its critics. Much research has pointed to the short-term nature of improvement which such intervention produced. Others went further and suggested that children could possibly be further handicapped by the strategies applied to assist them.

To counter this a much wider rôle is suggested involving such teachers in 'consultancy' work within schools, supporting staff with the production of materials and in the organisation of classrooms and suggesting teaching strategies across the range of curricular materials. Generally the emphasis is increasingly less on the withdrawal and remediation of the individual who is failing and more on the prevention of classroom failure itself. This development has been mirrored in the area of educational psychology. Many practitioners in this field now see themselves as much the organisers of new 'systems' for learning and the developers of schemes for the prevention of learning failure, as people whose function is to intervene on an individual basis. It is not that specialist skills with individuals are perceived as irrelevant, or never to be used again. Rather it is that the role of remedial specialist and educational psychologist alike is broadened to include the dissemination of successful pedagogic techniques and organisational models which have a more fundamental bearing on the lives of schools as well as on individual children. These trends are likely to reduce the number of children who are withdrawn from lessons and increase the number who either remain in, or actually join, humanities classes.

The view of the value of psychometrics as a helpful tool for teachers is also changing. There is a growing body of research which is highly critical of intelligence testing. For example, Moseley (1975) doubts that IQ can be a predictor of educational performance, and Leeming et al. (1979) considered that 'while intelligence tests may be of administrative value, they are of little direct use to the teacher in planning a programme suited to the child's specific needs'. Opinion, over recent years, has shifted to embrace the view that schools should not concern themselves too much with forces they can do nothing about. Increasingly teachers are urged not to hide behind the medical model which involved looking into the child for solutions to the problem. Instead they are urged to consider an approach which concentrates on those factors which teachers can do something about – the method of instruction, the objectives of the teacher and the classroom environment.

For teachers in the humanities the message is quite clear. When, for example, they are presented with children who cannot tell the difference between land and sea on a map of the world, or know which way up it goes, they are urged to ask themselves, before anything else, the basic question:

'What was it about what I did which meant that these children have not grasped the idea?'

rather than immediately to assume that the children did not grasp it because they have a low IQ.

If a ski instructor were to see a youthful and athletic head of humanities department prostrated and frustrated on the nursery slopes while all round him 9-year-olds showed much greater competence in performing the most basic of ski manoeuvres, the instructor might consider whether there was a language difficulty which resulted in the teacher continually getting his right knee in the wrong place. The instructor might consider whether he had failed to give the teacher the requisite confidence to conquer his fear of the slope. The instructor might give some thought to the possibility that the teacher's previous instructor had tried to teach the snow plough method not the more modern *ski evolutif* and that this was causing him great confusion. It is unlikely that he would doubt, or show much interest in, the teacher's IQ.

Subject teachers in the humanities are encouraged to consider, in a similar fashion, what it is that they do that causes some children not to succeed, to consider if there is a fault in the 'instructional system'. A scrutiny of resources, language, teaching style, content and task setting may reveal that different approaches would yield a much higher degree of success. Certainly to sit in the staffroom and complain about the 'basic intelligence' of the children is largely an unhelpful exercise. It is, after all, unlikely to improve 3C's map skills.

Teachers can be encouraged to look at the situation in a new way. Before considering what it is that 'they can't even ...', which is not unknown staffroom talk, teachers are urged to ask themselves whether the children have ever been taught the task in question. Children with learning difficulties are unlikely to profit from a view of education which sees it entirely as a process of osmosis. Children are capable of soaking up some skills, knowledge and attitudes that they are not directly taught, but the safest course for teachers to follow in their lessons is 'if they haven't been taught it, they probably won't know it'. As a geographer from Walsall has written: 'In preparing work for the less able pupils in the first year of the secondary school it is probably best to assume that they know very little.' She discovered, for example, that a group of the lowest achievers:

> did not know the meaning of the word daughter. This was not, as may be supposed a case of the pupils 'trying it on'. They really and truly had no idea. One or two had the vague notion that it was concerned with family relationships but to most of them it was totally incomprehensible. Such a word would not be used in their homes and it is unrealistic to expect them to understand it. When the meaning of the word had been explained to them their reaction was 'Oh, you mean the girl.'
>
> (Hitchon, 1982, p. 23)

In addition, the evidence is clear that children with learning difficulties, and some who apparently have none, are led into apparently careless errors simply because they do not fully understand what is expected of them. This does not mean that they will be successful even if they are fully aware of what is expected. It merely suggests that teachers have more chance to reach stated objectives if they are absolutely clear in their instructions. Practical strategies to achieve this are to be found in Chapter 5.

Also, some research has suggested that we need not close our minds as we once did to the possibility of teaching concepts to children with learning difficulties. The evidence suggests that if the way in which the concept is presented makes 'human sense', then children are capable of demonstrating that they have reached levels of development, in Piagetian terms, far in advance of their chronological age (Donaldson, 1978; Hughes, 1975). This is of great importance to humanities teachers since the essential core of humanities disciplines is conceptual. The suggestion is that if teachers package their concepts in a way which makes 'human sense', by the use, for example, of simulations close to the life of the child or that of the school with which the child is familiar, then that child is capable of achieving a greater degree of conceptual understanding than previously envisaged.

Another trend has important implications for humanities teachers. A significant number of those in the field of secondary education are coming to the view cited by Ingenkamp (1977): 'The only assessment that is educationally justifiable is that which

promotes the individual learning process.' Following a model
devised originally in the field of special education (see Chapter 3),
humanities teachers are encouraged to look critically at the use and
value of norm-referenced testing. They are urged instead, or at least
as well as, to consider the adoption of criterion-referenced testing.
To a certain extent these tests are diagnostic, i.e. they provide
information about where, if at all, the child is failing and provide
teachers with the necessary knowledge to suggest in what ways the
instructional techniques can be modified. They do not seek to
compare one child with another since that comparison cannot help
the child to learn, or give teachers any useful information. Perhaps,
the best explanation of criterion-referenced testing was given by
Popham and Husek (1969):

> We want to know how an individual can do, not how he stands in
> comparison with others. For example, the dog owner who wants to
> keep his dog in the back yard may give his dog a fence jumping test.
> The owner wants to find out how high the dog can jump, so that he
> can build a fence high enough to keep the dog in the yard. How the
> dog compares with other dogs is irrelevant.

To return to our athletic head of humanities, it is of no help to him
to know that everyone else in the ski class can parallel turn by the
end of their first week, while his attempt at the test ended in a net
overlooking a yawning abyss. All such a test is likely to do is to
confirm his belief that he would do better to sit by a fire during the
winter months with a book, waiting for better weather. Had his
instructor constructed a test which was attainable and designed to
show what his pupil had achieved *positively*, then the teacher might
have been prepared to try again the following year.

It is interesting that the essential principles on which GCSE are
based embrace criterion-referencing, and point to the eventual
abandoning of norm-referencing, although the plans have not yet
come to fruition in the humanities. The concept of 'differentiation'
in the GCSE places a responsibility upon teachers, in the design of
the internally assessed coursework, to ensure that every student
who sits the exam also does coursework which demonstrates what
they 'know, understand and can do'. It seems sensible that this new
approach in the 14–16 age group should be extended lower down
the school and that norm-referencing should gradually be replaced
by criterion-referenced testing. Indeed, we shall argue later that this
must occur if children with learning difficulties are to be catered for
adequately. The forms these tests take will have two great benefits.
Firstly, teachers should be able to use them to discover precisely
where children are failing and so be able to consider new

techniques. Secondly, teachers will run less risk of causing the motivation of their children to decline, because the tests measure what is known in a positive way, not, as with norm-referencing, merely continue to confirm failure and demonstrate to the children what they don't know, don't understand and can't do.

In conclusion 'remedial education' is moving away from the consideration solely of children who have been removed from ordinary mainstream lessons. It is becoming much more interested in methods of preventing learning failure by means of the adoption of a consultancy role within schools and by means of offering support within rather than outside the classroom. Psychometrics have, to a certain extent, been shown to be fallible as predictors of educational performance. Research in developmental psychology has suggested that humanities teachers can attempt the teaching of concepts to children who face learning difficulties with more confidence than previously. Testing procedures are gradually moving from norm-referencing to criterion-referencing. Equally, although sociological aspects of particular children's lives might suggest that they were likely to experience difficulties, none of these are of help to the teacher in the classroom since the teacher can do little about them. It is important for the teacher, especially the humanities teacher to know about these aspects for such knowledge is helpful for presenting material in a way which makes 'human sense' to the child, but they should not be used to provide justifications for teacher failure. Humanities teachers, then, are increasingly thrown more on their own resources. They are encouraged to examine their own work, and while they can expect more help from special needs departments, they are likely in the future to have more children with learning difficulties in their classes since the number of remedial withdrawal groups is likely to be reduced.

This is especially true since both the Warnock Report and the 1981 Act have attempted to push schools in the same direction. The Warnock Report sought to stress the responsibility of every teacher for children with special needs: 'it is imperative to realise that every teacher should appreciate that up to one child in five is likely to require some form of special educational help and that this may be provided not only in special schools and classes but also with suitable support in the regular classes of ordinary school' (DES, 1978). The message is quite clear. The climate of the times suggests that children with special needs are increasingly, and wherever possible, to be part of the general school community and that the responsibility of all teachers for such students' education is equally clear.

These students are not, in the future, to be pushed into a category which separates them from the rest in the class or the school, or be regarded as children for whom the 'normal' curriculum of the school is inappropriate. Children are to be seen as ranged on a continuum of abilities from those who are gifted to those who are slow learners; the slow learners are not inhabitants of different planets. It is not the children who are extraordinary or special, merely their needs. It is absurd to deny the proper educational opportunities to slow learners because they have been classified into an identifiable group by labelling. Schools require a much more positive approach to the education of slow learners. What is required is the belief that something better can be done.

REFERENCES

Ainscow, M. and Tweddle, D. (1977) Behavioural objectives and children with learning difficulties. *AEP Journal*, **4** (5), pp. 29–32.

Blank, M. (1973) *Teaching Learning in the Pre-School*. Columbus Ohio: Merrill.

Board of Education (1937) *The Education of Backward Children*. London: HMSO.

Booth, M. (1980) Teaching geography to lower ability children. *Teaching Geography*, **5** (3).

Bruner, J. S. (1966) *Towards a Theory of Instruction*. New York: Norton.

Ciesla, M. J. (1979) Geography and slow learners in the secondary school. *Remedial Education*, **14** (2), pp. 64–68.

DES (1971) *Slow Learners in Secondary Schools*. London: HMSO.

DES (1982) *Report of the Committee of Enquiry into the Teaching of Mathematics in Schools* (The Cockcroft Report). London: HMSO.

DES (1978) *Special Educational Needs*. London: HMSO.

Donaldson, M. (1978) *Children's Minds*. London: Fontana.

Folland, M. (1982) 'Using road networks'. In Boardman, D. (ed.) *Geography with Slow Learners*. Sheffield: The Geographical Association.

Gains, C. (1980) Remedial education in the 1980s. *Remedial Education*, **15** (1), pp. 5–9.

Galloway, D. (1985) *Schools, Pupils and Special Educational Needs*. London: Croom Helm.

Geographical Association (1982) *Teaching Geography to Less Able 11–14 Year Olds*. Sheffield: The Geographical Association.

Golby, M. and Gulliver, R. J. (1979) Whose remedies, whose ills? a critical review of remedial education. *Journal of Curriculum Studies*, **11**, pp. 137–147.

Gulliford, R. (1983) The teacher's own resources. *Remedial Education*, **18** (4).

Hitchon, B. (1982) 'The seasons with multi-ethnic groups'. In Boardman, D. (ed.) *Geography with Slow Learners*. Sheffield: The Geographical Association.

Hughes, M. (1975) 'Egocentricity in pre-school children.' Doctoral thesis: Edinburgh University.

ILEA (1984) *Improving Secondary Schools*. London: ILEA.

Ingenkamp, K. H. (1977) *Educational Assessment – European Trend Report on Educational Research*. Slough: NFER.

Leeming, K., Swann, W., Coupe, J. and Mittler, P. (1979) *Teaching Language and Communication to the Mentally Handicapped*. Schools Council Curriculum Bulletin No. 8. London: Evans/Methuen Educational.

Lloyd-Smith, M. (1979) The meaning of special units. *Socialism and Education*, **6** (ii), pp. 10–11.

Moseley, D. (1975) *Special Provision for Reading*. Slough: NFER.

Plowden Report (1967) *Children and Their Primary Schools*. Report of the Central Advisory Council for Education in England. London: HMSO.

Popham, W. J. and Husek, T. R. (1969) Implications of criterion-referenced measurement. *Journal of Educational Measurement*, **6**, pp. 1–9.

Widlake, P. (1975) The future in remedial education. Concluding remarks to NARE Conference, 1975 in *Remedial Education*, **10** (3), pp. 103–107.

—3—
The humanities curriculum – aims and implementation

In the course of the rest of this book we provide practical advice for teachers. We will demonstrate 'where to begin'. We will present ideas on the teaching of humanities that can be applied specifically to children with learning difficulties so that humanities lessons can be meaningful, enjoyable and provide a sense of achievement. We hope, in addition, that teachers as well as pupils will find lessons with these groups more profitable and capable of giving more job satisfaction. It is our experience that teachers do less well what they don't enjoy doing and, as Visser has pointed out 'teachers like children thrive on successful experiences' (1986, p. 7).

A necessary starting point is a consideration of why humanities should be taught to children with special educational needs. What does a study of this area of the curriculum have to offer? Why should humanities be included in the curriculum of children with learning difficulties?

WHY TEACH HUMANITIES TO CHILDREN WITH SPECIAL EDUCATIONAL NEEDS?

The justification for teaching humanities subjects to children with learning difficulties and other forms of special educational needs rests on two premises. In the first place educational thought has led to a theory of the curriculum which incorporates the concept of a 'core' which should be followed by all. Such a principle is the natural development of a long history of expanding opportunity in education in England and Wales. Demands for 'secondary education for all', which date from Tawney's work in the 1920s, the movement towards comprehensive education, recent concern for the issues of gender and race in education are all manifestations of it. Secondly, there is the notion that the study of humanities subjects, because of the nature of the disciplines, can be of particular benefit to children with special educational needs.

It is a central principle embodied in the Warnock Report that all children should follow the fullest curriculum possible and, as far as possible, all children should receive such extra help and aids, where appropriate, as to make this curriculum possible for them. The Fish Report set it out as follows:

> First and foremost special educational provision is now defined as the technology and methodology required to provide access for pupils with disabilities or significant difficulties, to the comprehensive curriculum and the emotional and social climate in which education takes place. These matters are the responsibility of all teachers not just those with specific duties in connection with meeting special educational needs, since **every** teacher is a teacher of such pupils.
> (ILEA, 1985, I.i.37)

It is this principle which lies behind the integration into mainstream schools and classes of some children who were previously set aside in special schools. It follows that if humanities subjects lie within an appropriate area of study for the highest achievers, then it is also an appropriate area for those for whom learning is more difficult. DES guidelines for curricular design in mainstream secondary education have acknowledged the place of humanities as an important area of experience. Within the general framework of the eight 'areas of experience', which encompass the aesthetic and creative, ethical, linguistic, mathematical, physical, scientific, social and political and the spiritual, humanities teaching has an important contribution to make. Some of these areas of experience are addressed in humanities teaching as part of the development of important skills without which humanities disciplines cannot be studied. Few, for example, would argue with the notion that the development of mapping skills in geography involves the use of important mathematical concepts in the development of competence in bearings, scale and contours. Equally they are involved in the use of histograms in work on demography in history or social science or of percentages in explaining the principle of proportional representation in the Weimar Republic.

Much of the work done in humanities departments must deal with important ethical issues such as racism, the relationship between the First and Third Worlds, or simply in biographical terms with the relationships between Elizabeth I and Mary, Queen of Scots. Similarly, other of the eight areas of experience such as the linguistic and scientific are approached in humanities lessons. While the major thrust of humanities teaching is in the direction of the physical, social, political and spiritual, imaginative and well thought out lessons in this area of the curriculum will encompass much more. The justification, though, for keeping humanities teaching in the secondary curriculum rests on the unique contribution which it has to make in the social, physical, political and spiritual spheres. This is likely to be the case for some time. As has been pointed out, most teachers have these eight areas of experience as delineated by the Inspectorate engraved as curricular commandments. No secondary school curriculum can be regarded as complete without some humanities teaching. All children are expected to leave school with some geographical, historical, religious and political perspectives.

It should be pointed out here that the introduction of various vocational and pre-vocational courses such as TVEI can have the effect of preventing children from studying a humanities subject beyond the age of fourteen. The last two years of compulsory education may have no humanities at all in them. This seems increasingly likely to occur: GCSE is not designed as an examination for the whole ability range. Claims that it is appropriate for the top 80 per cent seem, on inspection of syllabuses and draft examination papers in many subjects, to be widely overstated. Previously, when faced with a public examination system which took no account of the weakest potential candidates (the 'average' performance in this system across the entire school population at 16 was Grade 4 CSE), schools designed their own Mode III CSE syllabuses with this lower achieving population in mind. They tailored the course and the examination requirements to the needs of their pupils. This option has not entirely disappeared with the advent of GCSE, but the rules have changed to make it much more difficult.

Since GCSE is a centrally controlled examination, all draft Mode III syllabuses must conform, as the Mode I courses do, to the National Criteria and the General Criteria. Guidelines for teachers are contained in a booklet, *Mode III GCSE*, available from each of the five Examining Consortia. The task of writing a course and having it accepted by one of those consortia and the Secondary Examinations Council is daunting, and much more difficult than in the previous examination system. In any case, in the minds of some teachers, the whole point of writing a Mode III examination has been removed. These courses were written in the hope that something valuable could be studied by low achievers in their final two years of school and that success could be rewarded by certification at CSE, despite the fact that these students were unlikely to achieve anything at all at a Mode I level examination. The Mode III, in short, was intended to be an easier option, but still a valuable course of study. Within the GCSE framework, this option is not available. It is no longer possible to construct courses which are easier and still lead to the same final qualification. If the teacher and student believe that the student would not be able to gain the basic GCSE Grade – the Foundation or F Grade – in a Mode I GCSE, then, notionally, it is no longer possible to write a Mode III course which is capable of awarding that student that grade. No amount of tinkering with assessment techniques and the content of courses can disguise this fact. The school and the teacher are still left with the problem of what to do with the low achiever in the 14–16 age range so that this student's efforts can be rewarded positively.

To an extent, the whole philosophical basis of the GCSE collapses at this point. The essential ideal of the examination is to reward students' work in terms of positive achievement. However, as one of the GCSE Training Videos points out, 'candidates who do not reach the Foundation level will not receive a certificate'. This is tantamount to saying that some students, and in some schools this may be many, who follow a two-year course achieve nothing which can be recorded positively. The problems of motivation in classes which contain children with learning difficulties is likely to be great under this system. In the past it was usually possible to design the Mode III CSE in such a way that a student who was prepared to work hard and produce some work could have this recorded in the form, at least, of a Grade 5 CSE. This possibility is removed by GCSE.

Schools will, no doubt, discover a range of responses to these problems. Certainly, there is little evidence available, as yet, to suggest what curricular or organisational changes schools have made to overcome them. One possibility, however, is that there will be a greater proliferation of vocationally based courses for the 14–16-year-old and that many children will cease to follow courses in traditional subject disciplines, even of the integrated type, at the end of their third year in secondary schools. Students following these courses will not all have learning difficulties. Many who previously might have followed a traditional compartmentalised examination curriculum may well, if the option system allows them, find this arrangement more acceptable. This may be a major step forward in education although we should realise that it marks the end of the core curriculum at 14, and that not all of the areas of experience outlined by HMI will be pursued after this age by all pupils.

As we shall show in later chapters there is no reason why this should be so in terms of those areas offered uniquely by humanities teaching. There are other ways of recording achievements in the humanities than by GCSE certification, and it is possible for children with learning difficulties to achieve GCSE grades provided that sufficient thought is given to the problem of differentiation in the design of coursework and assignments. Moreover, humanities teachers have much to offer in terms of vocational courses which operate for this age group in school. Many of the concepts with which humanities teachers are concerned can be built into courses which have nothing to do with GCSE. If humanities departments cannot come to terms with the problems of the low achiever and cannot quickly address the challenge of presenting what they have to offer in packages which are not wrapped solely in traditional examination papers, it seems likely that their opportunities to present to children what they have to offer, will be reduced.

One major initiative in this area is the Manchester Modular Humanities Mode III GCSE scheme, shortly to become a Mode I NEA administered exam. This goes a long way towards solving the problem of what to do with low achievers in a GCSE context. There are several exciting features about the scheme. In the first instance it offers, as its title suggests, a modular approach to GCSE. Students or teachers select 5 modules for study over the two-year course. Depending on which combinations of modules have been selected, students may be awarded a GCSE with any of the following titles: history, geography, economics, industrial studies, religious studies, social science, humanities foundation course, community studies, local studies, modern studies, local studies, religion and society, or world studies. Notionally the breadth of choice is an important factor in producing strong motivation.

Of the marks for a GCSE grade using the Manchester modular system, 75 per cent come from coursework plus coursework tests and 25 per cent from an end of course exam. While there are some GCSEs in the humanities, for example integrated humanities, which are 100 per cent coursework assessed, the coursework in most syllabuses accounts for 50 per cent or less of the total mark. It has been argued for some time that internally assessed coursework is more appropriate for the low achiever than a high proportion of marks resting on the end of course examination. In addition, the very nature of this modular course is that each term's unit of work is self contained. Clearly defined targets which can be achieved over a term are tested within the term. The longer term acquisition of skills and concepts is tested at the end of the course. Moreover, it is possible to use the same piece of work to count towards a GCSE grade and towards a unit accreditation using the Northern Partnership for Records of Achievement. In practice, this means that the students can receive an official statement of what they have achieved in a term shortly after the end of that term. Unofficial comments from teachers involved in using this scheme suggest that there has been an increase in motivation. This is especially true of children who have not, in the past, found humanities subjects easy. (Details of this scheme can be obtained from the District Inspector for Humanities in Manchester or the Northern Examining Association.)

If we leave the 14–16 curriculum aside, it seems certain that all children will follow some courses in the humanities up to the end of the third year. This being the case, some of the benefits of studying humanities subjects must also be afforded to children with special needs. In schools we do not deal solely with an academic élite. Less than 10 per cent of the school population is destined for study in higher education. We cannot allow the design of the humanities curriculum to be decided solely by the demands of this small group. Other considerations must be met. We must consider what the needs of all the children are. It may be true, in a strict sense, that history is a discipline which cannot be properly studied only in schools. Nevertheless, in school we can approach the study of the past in a meaningful way for children. We may not be studying history as a doctoral student would recognise history, but it is not the function of secondary schools to award doctorates. We are engaged on the task of allowing children to move into adulthood with a range of skills, attitudes and knowledge which can provide them with personal and social competence.

In humanities lessons we are trying to provide children with the perceptions with which they can make sensible conclusions about the world as it was and, more importantly, the world as it is. Our primary aim is to give the whole school population the opportunity to develop a 'world view', to understand the workings of the world. If our generalisations and our models are sometimes crude and open to question in a strict academic sense, we need make no apology. Simply, schools exist for different reasons than do universities. They are not just one station along the road which leads to higher education, although they are for some. It is not sufficient, or true, to assume that humanities lie within the compass only of the average or above average child. As we shall demonstrate, children with learning difficulties are capable of the study of the 'essential components' of humanities subjects. They need not exist solely on a diet of basic skills in English and mathematics. If this were the case, humanities teachers would possess a philosophy which could lead to the decimation of their number.

If the existence of humanities in school is to be justified, then the fundamental experiences in terms of skills and knowledge which they have to offer must be accessible to the vast majority of children in mainstream schools. Each school needs to identify the 'core' of the humanities curriculum in its aims – those skills, concepts and attitudes which it deems appropriate for its children. Extra help, different resources and alternative teaching strategies may be required to assist some children to reach the objectives which the school has set for them within the core. How much help, what kind of resources and teaching strategies will depend very much on the different problems which particular aspects of the core present.

The department needs to define its baseline. It needs to decide what concepts, skills, attitudes and knowledge it intends to work on with all children who come into the department and then work towards achieving these with all. It is not necessary for each child fully to understand everything which is presented in school. Awareness of the existence of things which they may only understand incompletely is a vital component in children's ability to relate efficiently to their natural and social environment. To give an example of this in terms of humanities, it may be that some children would find great difficulty in understanding the process by which nuclear weapons work. Perhaps they find it difficult to remember whether the blast follows the flash or the wind. It is surely sufficient that only some children are able to sequence these phenomena. Few would argue that all children in mainstream schools need to be aware of the basic effects of nuclear warfare.

In addition, the study of humanities has benefits for children with learning difficulties which are connected with the nature of the humanities disciplines. The nature of many areas of content within humanities teaching transcend the benefits which can accrue in terms of skills, attitudes, concepts and knowledge. Both the Warnock Report and Brennan (1979) indicate that failure after school is often far more related to instability and immaturity in a social sense than to the students' level of academic attainment. Sound humanities teaching has a role to play in increasing maturity and stability. It can provide an overview of a particular child's life and development. The concept of a 'special curriculum' lacks credibility in a time when schools should be searching for an organisation which will pursue general aims. Even if this were not so, there are strong arguments which suggest that some humanities teaching should be an integral part of the curriculum for children with learning difficulties or disabilities even if other curricular areas are omitted. In practical terms this means that subject teachers within the humanities should be arguing to keep such children with them since their subject area has particular value. If children need to find time on the timetable for extra typewriting because, for example, they have a visual handicap and find writing almost impossible, then humanities teachers should try to ensure that it is not their lessons which are missed.

The study of differing types of people from different ages and different places can have the effect, if sensitively presented by the teacher, of improving the self image of the child with learning difficulties. As Bromwich and Bromwich (1982) have pointed out, the study of history can be especially useful in giving truants an improved self image. Their suggestion is that since history studies people at a distance, children can place their own behaviours in context and realise, without feeling threatened, that others in different times have also experienced problems. One of the present authors, for example, showed a video as part of a 16+ (now GCSE) course on modern history that was intended to demonstrate the changing nature of warfare. One of the compelling parts of this was the personal recollection of a British tank commander in the Second World War whose tank had been mined and caught fire. He described vividly the effects of the fire and the fact that his best friend who was manning the medical post did not recognise him when he was brought in. One of the members of this class was a girl who had been so severely burned in a house fire 9 years before that she had missed much of her education and was left badly disfigured. She lacked confidence and had found it difficult to make strong friendships in school. Since the teacher had admitted the girl to the school and had some pastoral responsibility for her in the past, he was able to discuss this film with her before the lesson and secure her agreement that she would be able to watch without embarrassment. After the end of the video and some discussion, the girl gave an account to the rest of the class of the years of treatment she had received. It was interesting to note that not only did the class discover in graphic detail the nature of some aspects of modern warfare but also it was possible to see the growth in confidence of the girl concerned and the growth of acceptance of her within the class from that moment.

This, of course, is only one isolated example, but frequently that is all a change of attitude, an increased perception or an improvement in motivation requires. Since we are not fully aware of all the problems which individual children have we cannot always predict what aspects of our lessons will have this effect. We believe that the scope for such 'accidental' and unplanned benefit is great because of the nature of much of the content of humanities lessons. Wilson (1985) reinforces the view of the importance of history as a vehicle of personal growth: 'History provides the richest storehouse of human experience and an unrivalled opportunity to reflect on other people's ideas and actions.' (p. 44) History lessons on rural depopulation after the beginning of industrialisation, for example, or on the plight of the handloom weavers in the first forty years of the nineteenth century, can often lead to children feeling less insecure and embarrassed about parental unemployment if the teacher has drawn the parallel between these events and the impact of technology in the late twentieth century. While we do not doubt the difficulty in the task of helping children to 'show an ability to look at events and issues from the perspective of people in the past', the process of working on this is an excellent medium for increasing the self knowledge and feelings of personal worth of our pupils.

Some aspects, then, of the study of humanities subjects can have positive effects on the self esteem of children. For children with learning difficulties the world becomes a less hostile and threatening place the more they can understand how it works. The contribution of good humanities teaching to this cannot be overstated. Wilson (1985) indicated that the study of history is important in the education of pupils with learning difficulty since it assists 'in developing a strong sense of social identity, awareness of past and appreciation of heritage, reinforced by visions of hope for the future'. If we accept Hargreaves's view of humanities teaching, that it 'promotes pupils' dignity and self esteem, to bring a sense of being worthy, or possessing creative, inventive and critical capacities, of having power to achieve personal and social change' (Hargreaves, 1982, p. 17), then we cannot argue that humanities teaching is inappropriate for children with learning difficulties. Rather, humanities teaching is vital for this group, since it provides them with knowledge, skills and concepts which are valuable for all but especially valuable for them. In addition to explaining the natural, social, economic, political and religious world in some way, humanities teaching can make major contributions towards personal understanding and growth. As Rollins (1985) suggests:

> Geography teachers can do much to help slow learning pupils to develop social and personal skills ... they can increase their pupils' self confidence and self awareness while leading them towards greater self reliance. They can also give their pupils much needed practical help as they move towards increasing maturity and prepare for the increasing complexities of life beyond the classroom.
>
> (p. 25)

The evidence from 'Project Heroes', a humanities curriculum programme in New York, is similar. Provided sufficient thought is given to the content and teaching method involved in the study of humanities, then this curricular area is well suited to foster a development of a sense of worth (Sharp, 1981). It is a curricular area which, well taught, can be a counselling tool. Children can learn about themselves to great benefit by comparisons with the situation of others separated from themselves by time or space.

AIMS AND SOME GENERAL OBJECTIVES IN THE DESIGN OF THE HUMANITIES CURRICULUM

Since the basic challenge teachers face is to access the core humanities curriculum to children with learning difficulties, it is appropriate here to include some comments on the aims and general objectives of humanities teaching. These comments are aimed at two main groups. Firstly, teachers who work within special needs departments and are interested in working with children in a supporting rôle within the humanities area, or who wish to advise their colleagues in that area, may find that educational thought there has changed since their last contact with it. Certainly (see Chapter 5) confusion can arise in the contact between humanities staff and the staff of the special needs department, simply because humanities teachers do not understand the nature of special needs and the special needs staff do not understand the nature of humanities teaching. This confusion may arise in relation to other subject areas as well. It may be that teachers with special educational needs responsibilities do not need to know about the whole curriculum and that, as indicated, it is sufficient for these teachers to know what questions to ask about teaching objectives, teaching styles and assessment techniques. However, an increase in the general level of curricular awareness can do nothing but good. As we shall suggest in future chapters, some research suggests that teachers in a support rôle are often at a loss in terms of the long-term aims and general objectives of courses with which they become involved. The ways in which the humanities curriculum has changed and a brief discussion of the general issues still under discussion may be of use to these teachers.

Secondly, there are many who work within humanities departments who are largely unaware of developments in other subject disciplines within the humanities area even though they might be entirely familiar with their own subject area. Unless a school presents an integrated humanities course, or a modular course where staff are expected to teach topics with which they may not, initially, have been familiar, there is no reason to assume that even history and geography teachers will be aware of the developments in each other's discipline. The structure of many options systems, which operate on the homogeneous principle, in the 14–16 age range, often dictates that teachers of history and geography are competing for students – not a situation best suited to produce harmony between them, and not a structure which is likely to produce dialogue and discussion about changes in curricular philosophy.

There are many aspects of humanities teaching which are unique. Frequently colleagues find it difficult to appreciate what it is that humanities teachers are trying to do. In the first instance we seem to have failed to have made our colleagues aware of the changes that have affected our work. It certainly is not safe to assume that staff from different departments will know of them. This is understandable. It is not realistic to assume that teachers have sufficient time to top up their knowledge of curricular areas other than their own when so much is happening in all parts of the school curriculum. How many humanities teachers, for example, will have read the Cockcroft Report on the teaching of mathematics? What goes on in other curricular areas is often cloaked in mystery, especially since it is also true that, traditionally, teachers have maintained an autonomy over their own classrooms so that the job of teaching becomes: 'like sexual activity ... seen as an intimate act which is most effectively and properly conducted when shrouded in privacy' (Hargreaves, 1980, p. 141).

In a time of rapid change if humanities staff wish to ensure that their colleagues know of recent developments then they have to tell them in staff discussions. It is not surprising, therefore, if some teachers assume that things are as they were when they were at school unless they see them differently for themselves. Many teachers are unaware of what is taught, and learned, in school, unless it is part of their own teaching or their own department. Deputy heads and head teachers may be aware of current trends although even this, through pressure of time, cannot be guaranteed. For many teachers in secondary schools the only knowledge they have of what goes on elsewhere in the school in curricular terms is what they see in the books of their tutorial group. They tend to presume that humanities courses are still based solely on content and if it seems that there is less concentration these days on dates in history and ox bow lakes in geography then these are two minor changes in what, in general terms, has remained the same.

Those involved in humanities teaching know that things are different. They know that they are concerned with human motivation, with asking questions, exploring evidence, problem-solving and the teaching and learning of generalised ideas and models – concepts. We also know how difficult this is. It is, for example, increasingly difficult for a non-specialist to set work for absent colleagues when that non-specialist has to take the group. Unless he or she understands the mores of the whole course and what it is we are trying to achieve then the lesson is likely to end in confusion. The remainder of this section, then, is not intended to prescribe a humanities course for use in secondary schools, nor even to suggest what may be covered in any of the disciplines which make up the humanities. It is intended to provide teachers with a brief description of some of the underlying principles of curricular design in the humanities.

To give an example from an HMI document on the teaching of geography, it is easily seen that expectations of the geography curriculum have been extended from those of even a few years

ago. These comments are concerned only with the *affective* do\
that concerned with attitudes:

> Geography offers the opportunity of situations where responsible
> efforts can be made to help pupils understand the nature of values
> and attitudes and their importance in making decisions. This is
> because social issues and matters of environmental concern which
> constitute much of the subject matter of geography, are clearly value
> laden … geography teachers should be endeavouring along with
> others, to encourage worthwhile attitudes towards learning such as
> respect for evidence, an awareness of biased reporting and intoler-
> ance, a suspicion of simplistic explanations, and a willingness to
> engage in rational discussion. Furthermore, geography teachers
> should be trying to ensure that their pupils develop an interest in
> other people and other places; have an appreciation of and sympathy
> for the life style and culture of others, including minority groups in
> our society; develop a concern for the quality of the environment,
> both urban and rural; are willing to consider other points of view and
> reach compromise solutions relating to proposed changes in the
> environment; are concerned with efforts to conserve scarce and
> valuable resources of all kinds (animals, plant, minerals, landscapes).
>
> (DES, 1978, p. 3)

A central aim of humanities subjects is to provide important
insights into human motivation. While this might be covered on the
school curriculum in some aspects of English teaching, it is in the
humanities that human motivation is most fully explored. Economic, social, personal, political, and religious motivation are fully
covered in the humanities as nowhere else. This is recognised in the
National Criteria for GCSE in all the individual subject areas. For
example, the National Criteria for Religious Studies indicate the
importance of recognising the relationship between religious beliefs
and values and the basic attitudes and norms of everyday life. In
geography, teachers are asked to consider in the design of their
courses the complex nature of people's relationships and interactions with their environment. In history, courses should promote
the acquisition of knowledge and understanding of human activity
in the past, linking it, where appropriate, with the present. All of
these are not solely intended to describe the aims of GCSE courses.
Rather they are statements of the aims of courses across the age
range in these subjects. In any case, the various National Criteria are
certain to have a profound effect on the content (and assessment
techniques) of courses throughout the secondary school. Few
teachers would argue that children with learning difficulties should
be deprived of a chance to discover those factors which make people
behave in particular ways, to discover the essence of being human.
Religious studies provide the opportunity for pupils to explore

religion through the practices, values and attitudes of people today. They are increasingly concerned with the study of the 'variety of responses to some of the fundamental questions which have always engaged people throughout the world at the deepest level' (SEC & OU, 1985, p. 7). Increasingly this discipline, as it is presented in schools, aims to address modern moral issues from a religious perspective and to examine the values raised by religious teachings. Older students in secondary schools may, for example, engage on a study of the moral issues raised by apartheid. There is less likelihood that they will simply be asked to explain a text. 'Good religious studies teachers have always encouraged their students to consider, for example, the implications and applications of the texts they have been studying, or to explore the meaning of worship rather than merely to label and identify the furnishings of a building used for worship.' (Op cit., p. 8.) There are clearly major challenges for those who teach children with learning difficulties in this different approach which concentrates on meaning and abstraction.

Apart from these central characteristics of cognitive aims, which are concerned with meaning and understanding of the relationships between people and those between people and the world, and those of affective aims which include a whole range of problems concerned with attitudes and values, humanities subjects also make claims for the development of a large number of skills. Among these are literacy, since so much of work done in school involves reading and writing, and the humanities subjects reinforce basic vocabulary and sentence construction as well as providing children with a range of language appropriate to the study of humanities subjects. The development of oral communication is an increasingly important aspect of humanities teaching since there is a much greater emphasis on oral work, through fieldwork in geography in the form of face-to-face survey work, in social science through investigative projects and in history through the growth of oral history. Also, there is a greater concentration on oral work within lessons, more discussion, more group work and a greater use of games and simulations which provide further opportunities for talking and listening. As we have seen above there are also many occasions when mathematical skills have to be used in the study of the humanities. Further, there are skills pertinent to the study of a large number of disciplines which make up the humanities. Mapping skills are important in this respect, developed in history, social science, and occasionally in religious studies, as well as in geography. Study skills concerned with the handling of evidence of a variety of forms are vital in the humanities – the development of the ability to locate and extract information from primary and secondary sources and to analyse and organise the information gained is an important aim of humanities teaching.

There has been a movement towards setting goals in terms of skills, attitudes and concepts, which are themselves aims for individual subjects for particular age groups. The HMI Series, specifically, *History Matters* has made great advances in this direction and has generated much discussion about 'progression' in history. The HMI book *History in the Primary and Secondary Years* (DES, 1985) is extremely useful for those who design courses in history. It provides a practical approach to the problem and makes pertinent suggestions as to general objectives. This approach sets out areas of study to which children should have been introduced by particular ages, in terms of skill development although not in terms of content. It gives lists of concepts with which children should be familiar by particular ages. This sort of model is likely to become more popular in an era which is moving towards a national curriculum. Equally, curriculum development in the humanities (e.g. time, place and society) has stressed the development of skills such as observation and communication at an early age and has embraced the idea that skills, attitudes and concepts need to be developed in a more sophisticated manner as the child becomes older and more sophisticated.

In geography, too, there is a trend in this direction. In an attempt to stimulate debate and to focus attention on a range of geographical activities which children might undertake at particular ages, various writers have proposed frameworks which might be adopted with, or without modification in secondary schools. Frequently the suggestions made are very general, noting, for example, that it is appropriate for children to study geography in a local, regional, national and international context. Very few make any attempt to identify and prescribe content.

The prevailing principle in modern humanities teaching is that content occupies a far less prominent position than previously. Content needs to be balanced against what has been studied before and what is to be studied later; all attempts should be made to ensure that the chosen content is interesting to children of the age group for which it is intended. However, there is less debate about what the content should actually be than there once was. Such a structure allows schools to use such resources as they have available and yet still cover the same range of skills and concepts. Perhaps this is the major change in the way humanities are organised in secondary schools. For humanities teachers who teach children with learning difficulties and for teachers who have a major responsibility for children with special needs the implications are clear. They no longer have the almost impossible task of thrusting vast amounts of factual content into children who find recall difficult. Increasingly, their task is to teach the fundamentals of the disciplines which make up the humanities in terms of conceptual understanding and a whole range of skills. This requires thorough planning and imagination, as well as the use of modified materials. Above all, it requires a structured approach and a knowledge of an appropriate instructional technique.

REFERENCES

Brennan, W. K. (1979) *Curricular Needs of Slow Learners*. Schools Council Working Paper 63. London: Evans/Methuen Educational.

Bromwich, A. and Bromwich, J. (1982) Teaching history to truants. *What Next?* **1** (4).

DES (1978) *Curriculum 11–16: Geography (HMI Geography Committee Working Paper)*. Birmingham: DES.

DES (1982) *Report of the Committee of Inquiry Into the Teaching of Mathematics in Schools* (The Cockcroft Report). London: HMSO.

DES (1985a) *History in the Primary and Secondary Years: An HMI View*. London: HMSO.

DES (1985b) *History Matters*. HMI Series. London: HMSO.

Hargreaves, D. H. (1980) 'The occupational culture of teachers'. In Woods, P. (ed.) *Teacher Strategies*. London: Croom Helm.

Hargreaves, D. H. (1982) *The Challenge for the Comprehensive School*. London: Routledge and Kegan Paul.

ILEA (1985) *Educational Opportunities For All? Report of the Committee Reviewing Provision to Meet Special Educational Needs*. (The Fish Report.) London: ILEA Centre for Learning Resources.

Rollins, G. (1985) 'Social skills and personal development'. In Corney, G. and Rawling, E. (eds) *Teaching Slow Learners through Geography*. Sheffield: The Geographical Association.

Secondary Examination Council and The Open University (1985a) *GCSE: A Guide for Teachers: Religious Studies*. Milton Keynes: The Open University Press.

Secondary Examination Council (1985b) *Mode III GCSE*. London: HMSO.

Secondary Examination Council (1985c) GCSE Training Video 1. London: HMSO.

Sharp, L. S. (1981) Project heroes: a humanities curriculum for the learning disabled. *Academic Therapy* **16**, (8).

Visser, J. (1986) Support: a description of the work of the SEN professional. *Support for Learning*, **1** (4).

Wilson, M. D. (1985) *History for Children with Learning Difficulties*. London: Hodder and Stoughton.

The practical implementation of the humanities curriculum

> Teachers who are prepared to spend time in planning structured, stimulating lessons are likely not only to boost the achievements of their pupils but also to gain greater personal satisfaction from their teaching.
>
> (Rollins, 1985)

The basic humanities curriculum should be, with extra help and modifications where necessary, accessible to all. Designers of the curriculum need to carry out their task with the interests of children with learning difficulties in mind. This should present few difficulties since the model we intend to follow is equally applicable to all children.

The comments of the secondary school teacher above summarise the most important point in the teaching of humanities subjects to children with learning difficulties. Her sentiments are, of course, also true for the highest achievers. In terms of achievements of children and satisfaction of teachers good preparation will bear fruit. All children merit well prepared lessons, but the level of preparation is much less important for the high achievers, for those who eventually will succeed in terms of high grades in GCSE. Children who rarely experience difficulty are quite capable of compensating for poor, or indifferent teaching. If the lesson is below par because the teacher is unwell, or because the teacher has heavy 'pastoral' responsibilities and is called to the telephone at intervals during the lesson, experience suggests that the high achievers will continue to remain 'on task' and many will continue to attain the lesson objectives. Even if the lesson has not been adequately prepared, high achievers may make up the deficiencies themselves. By private reading, or discussion after the lesson with each other, parents, older brothers or sisters many of these pupils will grasp whatever point their teacher failed to make to them. Many may already have been aware of the point in advance. They also are the children who are most likely to press the teacher to explain it again. Many of these characteristics are displayed by high achievers. As has been pointed out, most children learn through unplanned interaction with their surroundings as well as through being taught. It is a general characteristic of children with learning difficulties that they have a reduced capacity for unplanned, incidental learning.

These pupils will rarely compensate for indifferent teaching. For them, the teacher's preparation, and the direction given to them by the teacher during the lesson, is much more crucial. It is vital to their chances of success in school, and, as we have seen, success is vital to their sense of belonging, their self confidence and to their motivation. For these children the lesson may be the only opportunity which they will have for understanding a particular point. If the opportunity is lost it may not recur.

Teaching method is crucial to the amount which children with learning difficulties gain from lessons. The style of delivery of lectures in institutions of higher education, offering courses to well motivated, well qualified students, is likely to have less devastating effects. They may presume that their audience will not have learning difficulties and that a two-hour lecture is an acceptable teaching medium. Should some members of the class fail to understand or to grasp the essential points, then, notionally, deficiencies can be quickly removed by the students themselves by a perusal of the course reading list. Similarly, perhaps, some teachers in the humanities have taught 'A' level in this way, relying primarily on a didactic approach in which sixth form students made notes from what the teacher said. Perhaps such styles have not been absent from the 'O' level class room as well, at least until the arrival of the new courses at 16+ and GCSE.

Both authors remember exhortations to read, note and inwardly digest some piece of textbook history, as their history teachers were called away from their lessons. Such an approach stemmed from two beliefs. Firstly, teachers believed that children studying a discipline at this level would not have learning difficulties, or accepted that they would not pass the exam. Secondly, until recent times, humanities subjects, for all the talk and claims for conceptual understanding, were concerned with little more than knowledge and the ability to learn and regurgitate facts. Teaching methods of this type seemed, with some justification, to be entirely appropriate.

Clearly such approaches are unlikely to work where some conceptual understanding is expected or where a variety of skills are to be practised. They certainly lack efficacy with children who have learning difficulties. Very simply then, teachers of children with special needs have to be good. The skills required in the teaching of these students are more numerous and, arguably, at a higher level than those required to teach 'A' level. It is not true that teaching these groups or individuals is lower grade work, even though so often it is perceived as such. Rather, it is clear that the ability to reduce the content and skills of a humanities subject to its barest conceptual essentials so that it can be presented in an acceptable package to children with learning difficulties, is a skill of the highest level. As Bruner pointed out 'Good teaching that emphasises the structure of a subject is probably even more valuable for the less able student than for the gifted one, for it is the former rather than the latter who is most easily thrown off the track by poor teaching.' (Bruner, 1960, p. 9)

An appreciation of the structure of a humanities discipline is clearly required for those who teach the highest achievers in school. It is also required for those who teach children with learning difficulties. The ability to emphasise this structure is vital and demands considerable skill. It demands an awareness of the unique nature of the subject area, of the justifications for its inclusion in the school curriculum. Children with learning difficulties are usually more interested in these justifications than the high achievers, for whom the carrot of eventual examination success is often sufficient justification – justification by faith in the value of certification. The realisation that they are unlikely to receive these certificates comes to children with learning difficulties much earlier than is often assumed and frequently leads them to question the value of the courses they are expected to follow.

In addition, teaching children with learning difficulties demands a knowledge of how children learn in humanities subjects, not simply a knowledge of the subject. Teachers need a deep knowledge of what sort of material to present and how to present it, a knowledge, in short, of the instructional process.

The 'instructional process' we wish to commend is that based on objectives. Objectives are implicit in many human activities – a shopping expedition, a holiday, mending a car. For teaching they are vital. For many teachers they are implicit in their lessons. 'I'm doing Bismarck's foreign policy today' implies that children in the class will be given the opportunity to understand some of the complexities of nineteenth-century international relations. Alternatively 'I'm doing climate, today' implies that children will discover something about the weather. Closely questioned, teachers will present in detail their objectives for particular lessons, but usually, only if pressed. It is our contention that when teaching children with learning difficulties, this form of objective setting is insufficient. The framing of objectives in vague terms does not serve the needs of this population well. The objectives need to be tight, pertinent, justifiable, negotiated with colleagues and sometimes children.

Teaching through objectives is a method which has much to commend it to the whole ability range although it is especially useful for children with learning difficulties. There has been long discussion about this approach in humanities teaching since the publication of Bloom's *Taxonomy of Educational Objectives* (1956), which sought to set out behavioural goals for study. In 1971 the publication of Coltham and Fines pamphlet *Educational Objectives in History* attempted to view the study of history in terms of objectives. Serious reservations have been expressed about their use. For example, it can be claimed that the 'behavioural' objectives approach is not applicable to the discipline of history. While it is conceded that many of the skills that are required for the study of history, such as 'using the alphabetic system to locate items speedily', can be explained in terms of a behavioural approach, some teachers deny that specifically historical activities such as 'admitting doubt in the handling of material' is truly behavioural. It is suggested that the behavioural approach to history, cannot be justified in terms of the nature of the discipline.

> We agree that history teachers need to think very hard about what we are trying to achieve, but ... precise objectives of the kind required by Coltham and Fines are (at least) extremely difficult to formulate in History. ... We think that the full fledged behavioural objectives approach offers only spurious precision and that it is likely to do more harm than good by distorting history for the purposes of assessment.
> (Gard and Lee, 1978, pp. 36–37)

With regard to the use of objectives in geography teaching it is claimed by some authorities that attempts to predetermine the outcomes of study in some aspects of 'humanistic' geography do not take sufficient account of the nature of the subject. Objectives suggest the possibility of mastery. It is difficult to 'master' issues which involve attitudes or the complexities of interpersonal relationships.

There is no space here to enter a full discussion of the place of objectives in curriculum planning. We agree, however, with Wilson (1985) when he suggests that much of the discussion about objectives is semantic in nature. Our view closely mirrors his: 'No one could really disagree with a structured approach to teaching which emphasised carefully planned intervention on the part of the teacher to assist the child with learning problems' (p. 49).

Irrespective of the capacity of children for latent learning, teachers must approach the planning of what they actually want the children to learn in their lessons with precision. This is especially vital for children who have learning difficulties. To anyone who has marked a set of CSE papers in history or geography and seen what standard is reached by those candidates who achieved the 'average' grade 4, discussions of the philosophical nature of the study of history, geography, religious studies or other humanities subjects are of little value. To the classroom teacher or the special needs support teacher such questions are largely irrelevant to their everyday practice. What is required is an approach which takes into account the needs of their pupils. We know that the vast majority of our pupils are not going to become historians or geographers so, for us, discussions of the finer points of the study of these disciplines is not our first priority. We see such discussion as far removed from the everyday problems presented by schools and children.

Our intention is not to place teachers in a strait-jacket of objectives from which escape is impossible. Neither do we wish to fall into the trap of making lessons mechanical and dull because they have reduced a complicated issue to its essential principles. What we wish to do is to provide both teachers and pupils with the tools to succeed. We suggest that skills can and should be taught through the behavioural techniques of mastery learning, and that, where appropriate to the teaching of concepts and generalisations, this model should be used. What is currently being achieved by many pupils is of little value to them. If we lay ourselves open to the charge of reductionism, then we make no apology. So often is it the case that children are thrown into the medium of project work without the skills or perceptions necessary to cope with it. In the attempt to create a 'learning environment' at the expense of teaching, teachers have not acted in the best interest of students with learning difficulties. Children working on their own with unsuitable material, producing little of value in an inordinate length of time, is frequently the scenario witnessed by teachers who adopt these classroom strategies. If all the direction a child receives is 'do a project' on Elizabethan England or the life of Mohammed then this is the antithesis of the approach we advocate for children with learning difficulties. These children, above all others, need to be *taught* within a highly structured framework if they are to achieve success. At the very least this framework needs to be in the teacher's mind even if it is not always shared with the child.

The nature of humanities subjects in schools frequently raises difficulties in this direction. Lessons in humanities subjects are never content free. Even if the teacher is aiming at the mastery of a particular skill or concept this is usually achieved through the discussion of content. Even in lessons intended to raise questions concerning attitudes or feelings, these discussions are always centred on issues which frame the context of the lesson.

However, as we have seen, the nature of humanities content is such that it is possible to teach the same 'fundamentals' of a subject through widely differing contexts. In other words it is possible for a history teacher to approach the differences between 'primary' and 'secondary' evidence through a study of the available sources on King Arthur or through Richard III or through the Battle of the Somme. Equally, a geography teacher attempting to explain subsistence agriculture has a wide variety of examples from which to choose. There is danger in this. The wide choice of topics which can be taught often causes objectives to become muddled in the teacher's mind. Muddled objectives imply muddled teaching. Students with learning difficulties are unlikely to have positive learning outcomes under these circumstances.

There is a danger that humanities teachers do not refine what they want to teach sufficiently because they are sidetracked by issues involving content. There is less danger of this in other areas of the secondary curriculum. If a maths teacher were engaged upon the teaching of vectors, a science teacher on elasticity, a languages teacher on the imperfect tense, there might be some debate amongst colleagues as to the best method of teaching these aspects of the syllabus. Some teachers within these departments might express the view that a different approach could be more worth while for those who found these concepts difficult. What there would not be would be a dispute about what vectors, heat and the imperfect tense actually are. In the humanities, however, this is not the case. Humanities teachers would argue about what 'crime', 'sacrifice', 'the First World War', 'settlement', 'the Viking invasions', for example, actually are when they need to express them in terms of topics for study by children. Since none of these topics is finite, teachers find themselves engaged in discussions of the relative teaching value of certain aspects of them. Since they cannot study all the interrelated themes which make up 'crime' as a subject for study, humanities teachers are forced into a series of judgements about the essence of the topic.

There is then great divergence of opinion over what should be taught within individual topics. This is not only true between different education authorities and between schools within the same authority. It is true even within the same school and within the same department. Two teachers in the same school, with adjoining rooms and who are teaching the same 'topic' are likely to be handling their material in different ways, even if discussion about what to teach had taken more time than the actual teaching of it. When schools followed 'traditional' syllabuses in history and geography it was perhaps clearer to the teacher which method to use and there would have existed a fair measure of agreement on this. With the proliferation of syllabuses, methods, new ideas, discovery models of learning, a shift away from the concrete into 'ideas' especially in geography, this is less likely. To quote an example, for the purposes of discussion we asked two teachers from the same school to suggest ways in which they might tackle a subject common enough as an area of study in secondary schools: 'steam power' in the Industrial Revolution. We asked them to outline a classroom based lesson which they might attempt, and asked them what they hoped the children would understand at the end. Their responses led us to suggest that teachers who were intending to teach steam power as part of a course on the Industrial Revolution would have to address at least the following questions:

1. Is there to be a concentration during the lesson on the technical aspects of steam power? Is the intention to teach the children how the machine actually worked?
2. Is the teacher intending to concentrate instead on the separate condenser with which Watt adapted Newcomen's original engine?
3. Is there rather to be a concentration on the number of uses to which steam power was put, from the pumping of water in Cornish tin mines to attempts at the construction of steam aeroplanes?
4. Does the teacher wish to make a central point of the lesson the biographical details of the lives of Newcomen and Watt?
5. Is the teacher intending to stress the benefits of steam power in terms of transport, fresh food into the cities, increased production of British industry – then the workshop of the world – and the implications for Britain as a world power in the nineteenth century?
6. Does the teacher wish to use the lesson to talk about the connections between steam power and coal mines, the location of industry and therefore the growth of nineteenth-century towns and cities and the distribution of population?
7. Is the main emphasis to be upon the adverse social conditions which steam power created at the beginning of the industrial revolution?

Clearly teachers of the humanities would not necessarily agree about what the important aspects of steam power were. This is an example which is primarily historical although it does contain economic and geographical aspects. However, this is certainly not a problem which is confined to the study of history. In humanities, the possibilities for flexibility and interpretation of what is to be taught, without, for the moment, considering how the curricular objectives are to be reached, are far greater than they are elsewhere. Presumably, no teacher of the humanities would have it any other way. The problem is that, under pressure, teachers abrogate their pedagogic responsibilities and take the view of the writer of a particular textbook or worksheet, and unthinkingly and uncritically, 'do' steam power in the way the book does. This, clearly, can mean that material which may be inappropriate to the children in the group is used, or in some ways much more seriously, erroneous to the teaching points they wish to make.

These comments do not apply only to work with younger children in secondary schools. They apply equally to examination classes. While the GCSE lays out aims and assessment objectives rarely seen in previous examinations, the teacher is still left with considerable problems in deciding what points to bring out in particular lessons, both in terms of knowledge and in terms of understanding. To take one example from the Northern Examining Association's History Syllabus B in Modern World History, there is a section for study entitled 'Conflict and Conciliation'. Within this the knowledge required, and therefore, presumably, the understanding of that knowledge which is to be assessed by written examination, is set out like this:

(a)   Origins of Conflict

   (i)   Sarajevo and its consequences.
   (ii)   Causes of the Second World War
         Hitler's aims and expansionist policies: Appeasement; role of the USSR: Poland.
   (iii)   The Cold War
         East–West ideological gap; post-Second World War settlement; Russian expansion in Eastern Europe; Iron Curtain; NATO and Warsaw Pact.
   (iv)   The Arab–Israeli Conflict:
         Israel, Egypt and Nasser; PLO and its objectives.

(NEA, 1985, p. 4)

No two teachers of history would interpret what these syllabus requirements actually are in precisely the same way. The number of professional judgements involved in deciding what to teach are endless. The temptation to use a book which covers these topics in a, more or less, 'standard' way is great. The problem which this may cause is that the objectives of each lesson are swamped by the way the book handles the topic. Since the book is available the greater temptation is to avoid consideration of meaningful objectives at all. While high achievers may cope with this it is unlikely that children with learning difficulties will, even if they have one of the texts especially designed for 'lower ability' chil

Once teachers have overcome the problem of what to teach, they need to consider what pupil outcomes can be expected from their lessons, i.e. what the pupils will know, understand or be able to do as a result of the lesson. Curriculum is that which is learned, not that which is taught. This is the only meaningful definition. Consequently the syllabus, courses within it and, most importantly, individual lessons need to be subjected to the same rigorous questioning: 'Where am I trying to lead the pupils?' and 'How will I know when they've got there?'

In the setting of objectives for a particular course or lesson the following questions need to be addressed:

- Are the objectives real?
- Are the objectives relevant?
- Are the objectives rational?
- Are the objectives realistic?
- Can the objectives be defined operationally in terms of student behaviours?

This framework is largely taken from a model derived from Brennan (1979). We need to ensure that these questions receive positive answers, or we need to rethink the objectives. To take each in turn:

Are they real?

Do our goals relate to the long term or existing needs of the child? These are not necessarily the same. It is easier in almost all cases to achieve co-operation if children can perceive that the objective of the lesson relates directly to a need which they, at that time, perceive. AIDS Education may well be an example of this. However, it is frequently less easy to persuade children that what teachers perceive to be their long-term needs actually will exist in the future. Sometimes, even if they agree that this will be an objective that they should attain because it will help them in the future, the future seems a long way off. Even in these cases teachers should explain to children why they are being asked to do something during a lesson. Experience suggests that children need and appreciate explanations even if they cannot always agree.

In terms of humanities teaching and learning, the professional expertise of teachers must be the guiding factor. Theory regarding acceptable content can be referred to, checklists of skills may be useful, but, finally, it is the teacher's or the department's decision. It may be that a national curriculum will remove some of the flexibility here but for each lesson the question 'Why do I want my children to know/understand/do this?' will remain pre-eminent. If the teacher has difficulty in formulating a justification for studying a particular aspect of humanities then the objective is best abandoned. As Boardman (1986) put it:

> It is always important to think carefully about the objectives of a lesson before teaching it. We cannot hope to teach anything effectively unless we know *why* we are teaching it. We need to decide what kinds of educational benefits the pupils will derive from studying a particular topic. Careful thought about objectives will often affect everything else that is attempted in a lesson.
>
> (p. 27)

The process of deciding as to the reality of objectives is well described by Dilkes (1982) in relation to the planning of a course of work on the weather with a group of children who have learning difficulties:

> The first questions which I ask myself are: 'What do they need to know?' and 'Why?' My children, even with high teacher expectation, will not be pilots, ships' captains, or weathermen, nor will they be in a job that demands a high degree of technical knowledge of the weather. They will, nevertheless, be people who may enjoy a particular outdoor sport, such as football, cricket, fishing, tennis; grow their own vegetables or even farm; they will look at the weather forecast to see if tomorrow will be a good day for the family wash, a day out or a holiday. What is even more important, they will *talk* about the weather. They need to know, therefore, how to interpret the weather forecast on the television, from the radio or the newspapers. This can be the starting point.
>
> (p. 12)

After these sort of decisions have been made, teachers then need to consider how best to present them to their pupils. It is essential that they take every available opportunity to discuss children's learning with them and to explain why particular topics are being studied and why the teacher has set particular objectives. This is the question of relevance.

Are they relevant?

It is important, as far as possible, to believe that the children will see the purpose of the objective. This may not always be possible since they might have difficulty in appreciating some long-term goals. Nevertheless, it is useful for teachers to share with their classes the reasons for particular activities and to explain why a particular lesson is occurring at that moment in time. It increases the confidence of the learners if teachers appear to be working within a framework and to know what they are doing. Teachers who begin their lessons with: 'What you are going to understand/know/be able to do, by the end of this lesson is ... and it's important because ...' immediately give confidence to their pupils and purpose to the lesson. It is a much better opening than: 'What I want you to do today is ...' Explanations for the reasons for lessons are crucial in building a sense of worth and in giving children the impression that they are actually gaining skills, knowledge, concepts, and attitudes which are, and will be, of value to them. This is particularly the case with children who have learning difficulties. To an extent, these pupils should be involved in the decision-making process with respect to curriculum content i.e. they should understand the 'what' of 'what did you do today?' and they should understand the 'why' of what they did today. They need to know that what has been done was worth while and that they have experienced success in completing the task which was set.

Are they rational?

This is an extremely important area. It concerns whether the children have the pre-requisite skills to achieve the stated objectives. Pre-requisite skills, precisely defined, are those skills which are necessary to have any chance of success in reaching the next objective. For our purposes we define them simply as all those things which a child needs to know, understand, and do even to begin to cope with the demands our society will make of them.

Pre-skills (the usual shortened form of 'pre-requisite skills') are essential for any learning undertaken in secondary schools, irrespective of the age or achievement level of the group. How many times have teachers discussing proportional representation with a high achieving fifth year group found their lesson ending in confusion and in the realisation gained half way through the lesson that many of the pupils were unable to work out a percentage? They simply did not have the pre-skill to cope with the demands of the lesson. Equally, some children with learning difficulties have problems in reliably recognising left and right. Until they have reached mastery level in this, there is little point in a teacher trying to teach map co-ordinates. This does not mean that teachers should abandon these children to eternal ignorance of map co-ordinates. If the objective has already been tested against the two criteria of reality and relevance, then it is worth working towards and the teacher should seek strategies for providing the pupils with the pre-skill. A support teacher may be ideal in these circumstances, but, if one cannot be found, it remains the humanities teacher's responsibility to work out a teaching strategy and finally to ask for help from a special needs consultant elsewhere in the school. It is precisely at this time that the 'They can't even ...' comments start. Once this happens, failure, with all that it implies, is looming (see Chapter 2).

A useful exercise for humanities departments seeking to familiarise themselves with the importance of pre-skills is to take a standard lesson which teachers use yearly and list all the pre-skills they think are required. Sometimes the list seems endless and yet, always, some things are forgotten. Many of these skills are concerned with language and reading levels with which we deal in the next chapter but there are others, especially those concerned with reference skills, and background knowledge.

As we quoted in the first chapter, children who have never seen a river, or had explained to them what rivers are, i.e. the concept of a river, may be confused about them. Their understanding of the concept 'river' might end with the knowledge that it is a watery thing. They may not understand the idea of flow or the difference between rivers and canals. When asked to design and make a model of an island on which treasure could be buried, that must have mountains, a forest and a river, some first year secondary children made a model which showed the river 'flowing' from one side of the island to the other, thus creating a second island. They did not possess the pre-skill to achieve that objective of the lesson.

The purpose in giving thought to the pre-skills required for each lesson is to prevent failure. Much of the job of classroom teaching consists in going round the room helping children to achieve their objectives. It is helpful if the teacher knows what problems children are likely to experience in achieving the objective set, so that the short time for which the lesson lasts can be used effectively. It is useful to be prepared for these difficulties by predicting where stumbling blocks are likely to be. This can be achieved most effectively if the issue of pre-skills has been tackled first. For example, if a class was presented with a block graph which detailed casualties amongst the British population, both service and civilian, in the First and Second World Wars and a written question asked them to draw conclusions from the information, perhaps the main objective of the lesson would be for the children to be able to point out that there were less civilian casualties between 1914 and 1918 than there were in the Second World War because air attack was still in its infancy. If the group did not understand what the term 'to draw conclusions' meant then there could be some point in the teacher explaining this at the beginning rather than having to explain this individually later on. Lessons are relatively short. In many schools, for example, children would study only 120 hours of humanities subjects in a full school year. If children with learning difficulties are to get the best from their time in school, it has to be used effectively.

Initially, attempting to analyse 'what they need in order to cope with what I want them to do' can seem a daunting task. It is comforting, however, to realise that the task becomes easier as the teacher begins to identify more readily the sort of gaps in knowledge, experience, and skills children with learning difficulties are demonstrating. It also becomes easier as the problems of individuals are analysed. Moreover there is plenty of opportunity for an improvement in relations between teachers and children to take place.. Occasionally, perhaps frequently, teachers will under-estimate the skills of their pupils, which gives a chance for the child to say 'You don't have to tell me that. I know it already' – the child has been given a chance to demonstrate competence instead of failure.

A further benefit of realising the importance of pre-skills is that teachers can begin to construct units of study around them. Ideally, each new lesson should use skills which have already been taught and learned. In other words the pre-skills of the new lesson become some of the things which have been learned in the past. This approach has several important advantages. Firstly, it provides a measure of continuity in a curricular area where this is not always easily perceived by children. Secondly, it should reinforce what the children already know, and provide a further taste of success rather than failure. Thirdly, it serves as a quick measure of evaluation as to whether previously stated objectives have been reached. In many cases teachers will be able to discover if those things that they know have been learned are still with the pupils and can be recalled. Frequently a lesson, or a unit of work, is followed and a test completes the course. It is only in the end of year examination that teachers discover how much of what they were trying to get over has stuck. By building previously covered material into future lessons teachers can overcome this problem, and, if necessary, children can be encouraged to recover lost or hazily recalled information, skills or concepts. There is further advice on this in the section on 'learning to learn' at the end of this chapter.

Fourthly, this approach concentrates the mind of the teacher on the main focus of the objectives method. Teachers have to consider the value of what they are doing. They have to decide what to include from what has been taught into what is to be taught. There is nothing difficult or complicated about this. It may, for example, be a simple matter of building some important historical or geographical vocabulary which was learned in the last unit of work into the next unit.

If a department, at the beginning of a second year course, for example, had taught a unit under the title of 'What is History?' using as a basic resource parts of Jon Nichol's book of the same title, one of their objectives would probably have been that the children could demonstrate understanding of the crucial vocabulary regarding historical evidence. To build this vocabulary into the next unit, irrespective of its content, is an easy task. It simply means that the department's material on, for example, a 'patch study' of Elizabethan England would include tasks that demanded an understanding of the same words. In a classroom used by children with learning difficulties either as a segregated group or as members of a mixed ability class, these words would probably be displayed on the walls as representing crucial vocabulary to remind children of them and to act as a resource for future units (see Chapter 5). In geography, similarly, we would expect that any map skills that had been stated objectives in previous lessons would appear as pre-skills for some new objectives in future work in the department.

It should be pointed out that aspects of the 'new' geography and history lend themselves much more to this type of approach than did traditional methods in both disciplines. Purely content based courses do not lend themselves so easily since the study of one geographical area may have little in common with another and study of them, though approached much the same way, may allow little in terms of the deliberate incorporation of pre-skills. Similarly, in history there is little common to a study of medieval England and nineteenth-century Germany if the point of the study is solely to seek out factual information. However, new emphases on skills and concepts are much better suited to this approach, since both can be incorporated at will and can be overlaid on to a variety of content.

Are they realistic?

Teachers are encouraged to ensure that children can achieve the objectives in a short time. The importance of this is clear. As we have seen, children will respond to the sense of achievement which success brings. If tasks are too difficult or if they take too long to do, boredom and irritation are likely to occur. This often means that teachers have to change exercises in humanities lessons so that they are shorter. To an extent they become artificial, but they can still retain the essential principles. This is important for children who have learning difficulties for whom, as we have seen, concentration spans are often limited.

For example, if humanities teachers were explaining the nature of placenames as historical evidence they might give children two maps, OS or road maps, to work with. They might ask them to collect the evidence in terms of writing down all the placenames on the map, then identify those which had Saxon, Viking, or Roman endings. They then might ask the class to come to some conclusions about the nature of the settlements in those areas covered by the maps. The objective is rational but not realistic, simply because the act of collecting the evidence will take longer than the time for the lesson. The teacher, however, can make it realistic by splitting the class into groups and have each member of the group tackle a particular piece of the map, or have collected most of the evidence before the lesson and have made it available on photocopied sheets so that the children only have to spend a short time in collecting their part of the evidence. They see the way evidence is collected, they experienced the collection of a small part of it, and they still have time to reach the objective concerned with making conclusions within the time of the lesson. A great danger in setting objectives for children with learning difficulties, and this does not only apply within mixed ability classes, is that they do not work sufficiently quickly to attain the objectives. Teachers need to be sensitive to this issue. There are important implications for classroom management here. Teachers, for example, may need to decide the 'base level' objectives for all children in a class and then on 'extension objectives' for higher achievers within the same class. This is not easy to organise, but it is possible. Practical suggestions and room management strategies are discussed in Chapter 5.

Equally, it is important that the objectives set are not excessively difficult. Humanities lessons should be challenging and give a genuine sense of achievement for pupils, but they should not demand too much. To do so is to run the risk of shattering a child's confidence and the sense of trust that the child has built up regarding the teacher. Although designed for use in the teaching of basic skills to children with learning difficulties, Ainscow and Muncey (1981) neatly express the levels at which work should be presented:

1. Frustration Level:
   The child is making little progress towards achieving the objectives.
2. Instructional Level:
   The child is getting to grips with the objective although is still making errors. With the teachers' help the objective should be attained.
3. Independent Level:
   The child can perform the task with ease and makes few errors and is close to proficiency.

(Adapted from Ainscow and Muncey, p. 35.)

It is clearly in the interest of humanities teachers and humanities learners to ensure that the frustration level is avoided as far as possible. The SNAP materials, quoted above, were designed for use in primary schools, although the secondary version contains similar thoughts (Ainscow and Muncey, 1987). In secondary schools children who find themselves at the frustration level, as we have seen (see Chapter 2), are likely to find other interests in the humanities lesson much more quickly than they might have done in the primary school. In the planning stage tasks should be set which give a sense of achievement but which are attainable – sometimes a difficult balance. Chapter 6 on resources and the adapting of materials suggests methods which humanities teachers might use to avoid those of their children who have learning difficulties remaining at the frustration level. However, there are some general principles that can be applied which we consider here.

1. Identify what pre-skills are missing (if any) and provide them. This may sound completely unrealistic for a teacher facing a class of thirty students for the first time. As time passes and the teacher becomes familiar with the levels at which the students perform, the sorts of things each finds easy and the sorts of things some find difficult, the task of identifying missing pre-skills becomes much easier. Personal knowledge of the children can make a vast difference here.

2. Change the nature of the task by providing more concrete work if appropriate (see the section below on Teaching Concepts), or to break down the task into smaller steps. This latter strategy is known as task analysis. It is derived from a model which has been developed in special education and may not be extensively known in mainstream secondary schools. It is a model which is particularly useful in the teaching of skills although it can be used in relation to other aspects of humanities teaching. Task analysis is the process of breaking down a task into its component parts. It enables the teacher to look at a particular child who is failing, to discover at which stage of the task the difficulties are arising. Teachers analyse the steps which they are asking children to climb in order to reach the goal and when they reach the one which is not being mastered a different strategy is employed. If observation of the child reveals that the failure is occurring at a step which needed to be understood but which the teacher has not considered, the fault lies in the teacher's analysis of the task, not with

the child. We do not assume that the cause of failure is the child's inability. We assume that the failure is ours. We work from there to change our instructional techniques for the particular child.

A typical teaching problem for which task analysis is appropriate is in the teaching of grid reference on OS maps. This example (Figure 4.1) might be something which could be given to a group of children or it might be an example of task analysis which was only carried out in the teacher's mind. As Gulliford (1979) points out 'The crucial point is that the structure of the method, the sequence of the learning should be clearly in the teacher's head'.

```
                      MAKING GRID REFERENCES
  1.  Find the square on the map you want to give a grid reference for.
  2.  Put your finger on it.
  3.  Move your finger straight along to the left until you come to the next
      line.
  4.  Move your finger up or down that line until you find its number. This
      will be at the edge of the map.
  5.  Write that number down on your paper.
  6.  Find the square you want to give a grid reference for again.
  7.  Put your finger on it.
  8.  Move your finger straight down until you come to the next line.
  9.  Move your finger along the line until you find its number. This will be
      at the edge of the map.
 10.  Write it next to the one you've already written down.
```

Figure 4.1

While this sort of activity is amenable to task analysis, there are other aspects of humanities teaching which also are. History teachers might find it useful to analyse events in this way in teaching content where much happens quickly, as, for example, with the year of 1066. It is an appropriate method since it is not possible to understand fully what happened to precipitate William of Normandy's voyage to England, or why Harold Godwinson lost the battle of Hastings, if what had happened previously is not known. Analysis of the essential steps which led to these events, with the exclusion of events which are not crucial to the story, would be of great help to children with learning difficulties.

This process of task analysis is, of course, something which teachers do all the time. It is an essential pedagogical skill. However, it is useful with some complicated tasks to apply it systematically, actually writing the steps down and sharing this structure with children who have learning difficulties. It allows them to see that knowledge and skills can be placed into manageable frameworks.

Once the task has been analysed into small steps each step, if necessary, can be taught independently. It may be necessary with some individuals to insert additional steps. The approach must allow for flexibility for it is individual children that teachers teach not entirely homogeneous groups that do not change from year to year, or even week to week. When each of the small steps has been mastered then they come together so that the 'terminal' objective can be reached. Children with learning difficulties will sometimes require structured teaching to bring the steps together.

Task analysis is an excellent technique. As the teacher becomes more proficient at analysing tasks into an appropriate number of steps, fewer children will stumble. The attempt, however, to discover at what step an individual child is failing is expensive in time. Secondary schools rely on group instruction as the primary method of teaching. Individualised instruction is rare. There are obvious problems in spending a great deal of time with one child during a lesson to the exclusion of the rest. For a full discussion of this and for some practical strategies which teachers may wish to adopt, see Chapter 5.

In any case, to be optimistic, the number of occasions when the need for intervention occurs to deal with learning failure should be reduced as teachers become more experienced in handling this approach. Many difficulties will be overcome without recourse to strategies which require vast amounts of time. It has been suggested that the 'principle of parsimony' should be applied. This means first choosing the simplest, most obvious, least disruptive changes likely to bring about improvement in the pupil's learning. If the teacher is aware of the nature of the task and the steps to be followed, it is much more likely that the point of failure will be identified quickly and the difficulty overcome.

Can the objectives be defined operationally in terms of pupil behaviours?

As we have seen, some humanities teaching does not lend itself to a behavioural objectives approach. A history teacher may wish to play some polyphonic music to a class to demonstrate the sort of music which sixteenth-century English kings and queens may have enjoyed. It is difficult to set an objective which will define what children will be able to do, say, write or draw as a result of having listened to it. This does not mean to say that the activity is a waste of time or that it should not be pursued. There is clearly value in it for its own sake. The objective is simply that the class should listen to the music but this is not a behavioural objective. It is rather an 'expressive objective' in which the teacher sets up what has been termed an 'educational encounter' where the situation is evocative but not prescriptive. Some of humanities teaching and learning falls into this category; most of it, however, does not. Most of it can be defined in behavioural terms where the teacher can state precisely what the children will be able to do as a result of teaching. Wherever the teaching situation is amenable to this, the behavioural objectives approach should be used.

EXTENDING THE OBJECTIVES APPROACH

When the process of setting objectives for children with learning difficulties is understood and can be applied to individual lessons, departments may wish to look at extending this approach. They may find it useful to express more of their work with this population in terms of objectives. An interesting model for this is provided by McCall (1982). He argues that if departments defined carefully what is taught in terms of objectives then it would be possible to concentrate on learning to learn objectives as primarily more important than the learning of specific information. The point behind such an argument is that most children, with the best instruction, will not remember much *factual* information, in terms of historical or geographical knowledge. If they can remember how to approach historical and geographical problems and have some conceptual understanding then their time in school has been more worth while. Moreover, he argues that 'where teaching intentions are explicitly stated there is an increase in opportunity for curriculum based assessment, that is, the progress of individual children monitored against specific criteria' (p. 13).

The example he presents is a topic outline from a third year history syllabus shown in Figure 4.2.

Traditionally, this topic of study would be taught by teachers and subject to the same problems indicated above. Among these would be (1) the teachers would not really know that they wanted to come out of the study, and (2) they would have no method, except in an impressionistic sense, of knowing what they had achieved at the end of it. There may have been a test which completed the topic but this would, most likely, have tested content only, which in a few weeks or months would have been largely forgotten by the majority of the pupils.

Third-year history syllabus (chosen extract – The English Overseas: in India). Syllabus as presented reads:

Topic outline – in India
The European traders – Portugal, France and England in India
Formation of the British East India Company
Rivalry between France and England
India at the time of Clive

Story of Clive of India
Black Hole of Calcutta
Battle of Plassey
Reference to India today in relationship with the U.K.

Source: Colin McCall 'Some National Reports and Surveys'. In M. Hinson and M. Hughes (eds) *Planning Effective Progress* (Amersham, Hulton Educational, 1982).

Figure 4.2

McCall suggests that the staff look at this outline and clarify their specific teaching intentions. In his outline this is a task which is performed by 'remedial' specialists. With practice, however, there is no reason why humanities departments themselves cannot undertake this work of expressing the nature of the content in terms of observable final results in students. A suggested framework of what their efforts might yield is shown in Figure 4.3.

Some of these learning outcomes are not strictly behavioural, in that 'appreciates some of the trials and tribulations faced by: ordinary people, and the leading personalities during this period' cannot be observed by the teacher, since appreciation cannot readily be measured. Nevertheless, this example does demonstrate the sort of approach which we commend. It identifies those things which the teacher is intending the child to learn and expresses them largely in terms of measurable objectives.

In summary, to ignore the objectives approach with children with learning difficulties is to serve them badly. Objectives provide a structure in a curricular area which has often lacked one. The approach concentrates the minds of teachers as they take on the task of both curriculum and lesson planning. It ensures that, at least, what teachers want children with learning difficulties to get out of their lessons is well defined. This is crucial for, as Mager (1962) pointed out, 'If you're not sure where you're going, you are likely to end up some place else – and not even know it.'

Assessment

For teachers to assume that what has been taught has necessarily been learned is patently absurd. In a lesson without explicit objectives it is possible to be content if a test on the topic reveals that

Stage B – statement of learning outcomes.
The following can be the behavioural objectives (a sample drawn from a larger sequence) for a pupil doing this unit of work:

Topic outline – the English Overseas: in India

Learning-to-learn objectives
Identifies differences between pictures, charts, graphs, maps, etc., and distinguishes appropriate use.

Understands written comprehension questions and responds with appropriate reading strategy.

Given a selection of major reference sources, identifies three appropriate to a given assignment and orders them in terms of priority.

Uses contents table and index when locating information.

Demonstrates competence in the use of a variety of writing and drawing implements.

Uses following equipment effectively: compass, simple camera, tape-recorder, atlas, film-strip.

Demonstrates appropriate use of the school library classification system.

Compiles short statements summarizing a text.

Demonstrates elementary competence at note-taking.

Demonstrates elementary skill in critical evaluation.

Demonstrates a rough notion of chronology using: ladder, pie-chart indicator, sequence of important events.

Content objectives
Identifies two influences on modern life from this historical period.

Can name three major personalities and relate basic facts associated with them.

Can think of, etc. modern counterparts of these three historical figures.

Draws a simple sketch of India and locates key places.

Draws and reads a simple relief map of India.

Can name main differences between major religions practised in India and other world religions.

Spells correctly and knows appropriate meaning for the following key vocabulary: India, ruled, power, century, British, French, trade, rivalry, conquered, princes, Bengal, Plassey.

Knows Sanskrit equivalent for five common English words.

Appreciates some of the trials and tribulations faced by: ordinary people, and the leading personalities during this period.

Source: Colin McCall, 'Some National Reports and Surveys'. In M. Hinson and M. Hughes (eds) *Planning Effective Progress* (Amersham, Hulton Educational, 1982).

Figure 4.3

only half the class has remembered half of the lesson. It can be justified in terms of the ability of the children, their behaviour during the lesson, the complexity of the topic as presented in the textbook or source material and even in terms of the fact that in the previous year a similar class did less well. The lesson which is based on objectives, however, has no such justification open to it. If only 50 per cent grasped the ideas, there was something wrong with the lesson – the objectives were unrealistic, the test did not adequately assess the stated objectives, the children were bored because the material was badly presented, or the teacher was having an off day.

Implicit in this whole discussion of objectives is the notion of assessment. To an extent there is no point in thinking of objectives unless some attempt is made to discover whether they have been reached or not. Since an educational objective is a statement about what a child will be able to do as a result of teaching which is received, it is clear that the teacher must be able to assess whether the objective has been achieved. We accept the reservations that some aspects of the study of history are not amenable to the setting of behavioural objectives. We would agree that this is also true of some aspects of geography, social science, and religious studies. Despite this, it is still true that many aspects of these disciplines in secondary school can be taught by using the behavioural objectives approach.

Assessment of children frequently implies IQ testing, tests of reading age, and other normative tests. This, for the reasons set out in Chapter 2, is not the sort of testing in which we are primarily interested. Neither are we interested in ipsative assessment, that which measures a student's performance against their previous performances: while this is a useful model for recording change and progress, which we do commend, it is difficult to design a curriculum document around it, when all the teacher has to work with is a student's previous performance. Moreover, the inherent danger of the ipsative approach is that it can lack rigour and deny that there are certain skills, attitudes and values which it is useful for everyone to possess. It can lead teachers away from these essentials into teaching which is entirely based on what students have been able to do previously. To an extent, the task of considering how best to approach a topic which may be difficult is no longer relevant under an ipsative approach. The temptation is to ignore possibly difficult ideas and concepts on the basis that because particular students have not performed very well in the past they will not perform well in the future.

Essentially this is merely a manifestation of the 'top–down/bottom–up' debate. The 'top–down' takes as its starting point an established body of knowledge, ideas, skills, concepts and attitudes and teaches those, sometimes irrespective of the response of the students or their ability to handle them. The 'bottom–up' approach takes as its baseline what the students can do and designs the subsequent curriculum around that. In assessment terms, normative testing tends to accompany the top–down orientation, while ipsative testing goes along with the bottom–up approach.

In this debate we take a middle position. Humanities departments must attempt to decide what is important and try to access all children to that. In doing so they also need to take greater account of what the students have already achieved. The objectives model set out above and a system of assessment based, primarily, on criterion–referenced testing fulfil both these goals. If our objectives have survived when placed against the criteria of what have been called the 'four Rs' – Reality, Relevance, Rationality and Realism – plus Operationalism, then these are objectives which our children should reach. Our task as teachers is to ensure that they do. Assessment for us is nothing more, then, than discovering if we have been successful in our teaching, and by implication whether the children have been successful in their learning, i.e. whether they have reached the stated objectives. This type of assessment procedure is known as criterion–referenced assessment. It is alternatively known as domain–referenced testing or objectives referencing. It involves discovering how well a child has done in comparison with some previously stated criterion, rather than how well that child has done in comparison with other children.

To be of use to teachers, assessment procedures should reveal where the children are succeeding and where they are not. The assessments need to be *diagnostic* in character so that they can provide information which can then be fed back into the process of task analysis or into the setting of new objectives. Traditional methods such as standardised testing have not done this adequately. They have had the effect of comparing individual children against a 'norm', which might in some cases be produced by a comparison with the mean in a class test or in others by comparison with previous years which attempted the same test. For the child with learning difficulties these tests are of little value. Many schools will continue to use them, but they should be used sparingly. Children seem to want to know how they are doing in comparison with others. They have models of league tables in football and other sports to follow. However, teachers should try to steer students away from the view that doing better than the person sitting next to them means that they are learning all they could or from the view that doing worse means that they should abandon hope.

There needs to be a dynamic relationship between testing and the curriculum. This is the whole point of criterion–referenced testing methods. Humanities teachers who use the same end of term test or end of year examination year after year, until the syllabus changes, are not serving the needs of pupils with learning difficulties and are ensuring a sterile curriculum.

There are many justifications for the more recent approaches to assessment. Some of them are well documented by Muncey and Ainscow (1983). Information gained from assessment is specific and has direct implications for teaching. Programmes using objectives can facilitate continuous assessment and review. The philosophy behind the approach is essentially optimistic in the sense that where children do not learn, there is assumed to be a flaw in the instructional design, not the child.

To a certain extent, however, the greatest justification for the use of criterion–referenced assessment is simply the effect that norm-referencing has on children with learning difficulties. Until the arrival of GCSE, one of the functions of public examinations was to separate achievers from non-achievers. Schools and humanities departments were not immune from this, and mirrored what happened at 16 at younger ages, by administering a variety of tests or examinations. Of necessity, some children did very well and some did very badly. Lists of results appeared on classroom walls and doors, percentages appeared, sometimes with position in classes or groups, on reports which were sent home to parents. How parents were supposed to interpret 37 per cent, 7th/31, is impossible to say. Testing of this type became part of the mythology of English education, as if the essential point of being in school was competition. Moreover, within schools, tests were often accorded a status they simply did not deserve. They claimed to be testing certain aspects of, for example, history or geography, whereas in reality they tested little more than the skill of comprehension, factual recall or the ability to set out work neatly. These are important skills but in no sense are they the only skills which humanities subjects are supposed to develop. They were used as tools which provided information for setting, or streaming, and for practice 'for the real thing'. When pressed to consider the validity of the exercise, teachers simply could not see why they had set them.

The greatest casualties in this periodic assessment procedure were, and are, the children with learning difficulties. Through a slow pace of work, a lack of understanding of what was required in the test, poor recall of what had been taught and a variety of other reasons, they failed, and began to take on the manifestation of self-perceived inadequacy. Since tests are usually written, children whose writing ability is poor are penalised. Frequently, children who understood, for example, the relationship between trade and transport structure were unable to show it through the absence of writing skills. In some countries students may request oral tests. In the USSR these are the norm. Traditionally this has not been the case in the schools of England and Wales.

Frequently, lower school humanities teachers modelled their tests and end of year exams on CSE, 'O' level or 16+ papers. Since by definition, children with learning difficulties could not pass these at 16, they were unlikely to do well on those designed for younger children either. Teachers would attempt to soften the blow with such platitudes as 'That's good ... for you', or 'I wouldn't worry about that. The test shows that you can do some of it.' Attempts to disguise the meaning of results to children usually fail. They know that their result is a statement of their worth, and that they are not worth very much.

Tests should not be set unless the teacher has a clear purpose in mind. Tests should assess whether children have reached the stated objectives and therefore *directly affect subsequent teaching*.

An important piece of research in Scotland has some very positive findings in this respect. The Schools' Assessment Research and Support Unit (1984) of the SCRE undertook a project on criterion–referenced assessment in the classroom, and among its findings were those now shown below. They are especially pertinent since some of the teachers interviewed were using *A Diagnostic Resource in Geography* (Black and Goring, 1983).

- The motivation of pupils increased.
- Pupils became aware much more easily of their own strengths and weaknesses since they knew what objectives they were aiming for and understood the results of their assessment.
- Pupils seemed more willing to ask for help when it was needed.
- Diagnostic testing did not seem to have detrimental effects on teaching but rather encouraged greater emphasis in dealing with the needs of individual pupils and 'stretching' them if they had already achieved the core.
- Pupils could appreciate that the tests were *formative* and that as an aid to learning they were much more interested in becoming involved.
- Diagnostic testing does not take any longer than conventional testing once teachers have some experience of the approach.
- No evidence was found to suggest that this form of assessment had a detrimental impact on classroom management.

It is interesting, and perhaps demonstrates how deeply ingrained norm–referencing is, that children however, were still keen to know how they were doing relative to others in the class. The researchers suggest that children need to be taught how to regard criterion–referenced feedback.

As the Scottish team pointed out (1984), 'teachers may increasingly want to turn to diagnostic assessment to trace their pupils' progress towards the criteria set out for external examinations, as well as using the approach lower down the school'. This is not only true in Scotland. The introduction of the GCSE in England and Wales with the intention to move towards criterion–referenced testing is a major and welcome step towards a more rational approach to assessment. Coupled with the movement in some pre-vocational courses, and in some LEAs towards profiling, the GCSE is an important initiative towards teaching of objectives and assessing by criterion–referencing. In terms of assessment in the humanities the implications are clear. Tests need to be designed which assess whether children have reached the stated objective. It should be repeated here that to be truly behavioural, the test must be one that gives an opportunity for children to demonstrate in an observable way whether they have reached the objective, i.e. by saying, writing, drawing, or doing.

For instance, in the example task analysed above (Figure 4.1), the terminal objective was to describe a square on a map in terms of a four figure grid reference. The criterion for mastery of this task would be that the child would describe a square correctly on three occasions. It might be that we would have to test this again in the future to ensure that the child still possessed the skill, but we would probably do this, as described above, by building it in as a pre-skill of some future activity. The circumstances under which this test might be conducted would vary. In some classrooms it would be done by teacher observation. The teacher would walk round the room to see who had reached the objective.

In this process we see another difference between criterion–referencing and norm–referencing. A traditional requirement for the normative test is for it to be conducted in silence. Frequently, this is for no other reason than that to talk might mean that someone is cheating and to cheat is to gain an unfair advantage over someone else. The criterion–reference test need not operate under this constraint. Its purpose is to improve the quality of teaching and therefore the quality of learning. If a teacher can explain the task again and help a child to reach criterion during the 'test', this is all to the good, for this is the purpose of the assessment. It is not a competition other than the student against the criterion. The point of a competition is that there are only a few prizes. In criterion–referenced approaches everyone can succeed in an absolute sense, and should be encouraged to do so. Certainly in the younger end of a secondary school it is possible for humanities teachers who adopt this approach to change radically the way in which they represent the progress of the children to the children themselves. If the element of between-child competition is taken from the lesson and the test there should be benefits for all.

The purpose of assignments and tests should be shared with classes in the same way the objectives of lessons should be shared. Children can be put at their ease and can be encouraged to be honest with regard to tests, if the teacher makes the point, frequently, that the test is for everyone's benefit. It can help if teachers make the evaluation of their work the prime purpose of the test. Classes respond to 'We're going to have a short test. I'm not writing the results down but I want to see how well I've taught the lesson.' This is an excellent way of securing co-operation and the correct attitude of the children to testing. After all, under the objectives approach this is precisely what the teacher is doing. Assessment of the children is evaluation for the teacher, evaluation of the curriculum, the method and the resources. It is in everybody's interest that the children have understood the points the lesson was trying to make.

Moreover, the criterion–referenced approach gives a much more valuable picture, or profile, of a child. It is possible with sensible record keeping to be able to present a profile of a child's achievement in humanities lessons which is available for discussion at Parents' Evenings and used to make pertinent remarks on written reports. Systems to achieve this will vary but the main purpose is to design a system where the objectives which each child has reached are recorded. In other words teachers should be recording from the first year the things which children 'know, understand, and can do'.

Teachers need also to be aware that even when they are not testing to discover if objectives have been reached each piece of work which children do is a guide to how far they are towards reaching those objectives. Classwork and homework needs to be marked with this in mind. Meaningless marks like 9/10 or As, Bs and Cs should be avoided. They serve little purpose, especially in many humanities lessons. It may be appropriate to award a mark out of ten if there are ten factual questions. It may be appropriate to mark in this way on a task concerned with map symbols. It is, however, not appropriate for pieces of ordinary classwork which children have completed. A comment, including suggestions for improvement, is much more sensible. This is, of course, especially true for the children with learning difficulties for whom, unless there is a whole school policy along these lines, the school week is likely to be littered with low marks.

The problem of allowing all children to show in the GCSE what they 'know, understand, and can do' has concentrated minds on the problem of assessment at 16. One of the solutions to this is 'differentiation by outcome'. We wish to explore this, briefly, for it has many applications for humanities teachers both in the 14–16 age group and with younger children. Essentially, differentiation by outcome means that all children, irrespective of competence, are asked the same question and on the way in which they answer it depends the final mark for that question. An example is given which was used in the *Teacher's Guide for History* (SEC and the OU, 1985):

> At the age of 17 John Smith volunteered for the army. In July 1916 Private John Smith was decorated for bravery during the battle of the Somme. Early in 1917 he was court-martialled and executed for cowardice.
>
> How might you explain John Smith's attitude to the war on the Western Front from the time he volunteered to the date when he was court-martialled?
>
> *Mark Scheme*
>
> What follows is admittedly crude, but offers an illustration of the sorts of levels of response which might be created.
>
> Level 1: Sees the events – volunteering, being decorated, being shot – as disconnected; offers valid explanations of each, but makes no attempt to view them as part of a whole.
>
> Level 2: Attempts a holistic approach but subsumes events under one set of feelings – loyalty, bravery, fear, horror – which have only partial explanatory power.
>
> Level 3: Reconciles apparently divergent behaviour by recognising that feelings may be aroused/modified in the light of experience, and that whilst John Smith's feelings may be all of a piece they might be given a number of different labels at different times.
>
> Level 4: Additionally recognises that from the outside observer's (e.g. the historian's) standpoint ascription of motives can never be more than tentative.

This is precisely the sort of question which does not readily fit the behavioural model. The candidate, as would be the case in religious studies and geography, is asked to deal with attitudes and human motivation. It is difficult to write objectives for this sort of question since it is not easy to predict the outcomes of such questions. However, the mark scheme in this example does provide clues as to the possible ways in which teachers might approach these areas. With this type of humanities issue teachers are encouraged to consider 'levels of responses'. This involves setting objectives at different levels of difficulty, and considering from what the children produce which level they have reached. This idea is manifested in a general way in the grade descriptions at GCSE. For example, in religious studies, a candidate who had reached the Foundation (F), level would have demonstrated:

> a partial knowledge of the syllabus content; this implies an ability to select some of the relevant information required and to set it down with an attempt at organising the material.
> such understanding of some of the areas concerned with the study of religion as will demonstrate, for example, an ability to:-
> (1) recognise particular uses of language in religion.
> (2) explain in simple terms the influence of special people, writings or traditions.
> (3) state a principal religious belief in their own words.
> (4) recognise a moral issue and to relate an appropriate religious belief to it.
> (5) recognise a question about the meaning of life and link it to the study of religion.
>> (GCSE. National criteria. Religious studies, 1985, p. 4)

Candidates who were to be awarded a grade C, on the other hand, would be likely to have demonstrated a higher level of what they know, understand and can do, i.e. they should show:

> a wide knowledge of the syllabus content: this implies an ability to select some of the salient features of the information required, to identify contexts and to show some skill in organising and presenting the material.
> a reasonable understanding of most of the areas concerned with the study of religion and in particular:-
> (1) a correct understanding of some uses of language in religion, including a simple understanding of basic concepts.
> (2) some understanding of the influence of at least one of the examples (special people, writings, traditions) on individuals or religious communities.
> (3) an ability to explain principal beliefs clearly and to trace a relationship between belief and practice.
> (4) a clear understanding of at least one moral issue and the application of a religious belief to it.
> (5) an ability to identify and to respond independently to a question about the fundamental meaning of life which might evoke faith responses.

This approach to assessment is not without difficulty as the example demonstrates. In realistic and practical terms it is often difficult to decide what kind of performance would distinguish one grade from another. This is a difficulty shared by profiling when it is frequently difficult to decide which comment on a checklist or from a comment bank best describes what a child has done. Both of these techniques of assessment are still fairly new. Teachers clearly need much practice in their use. Though they may present difficulties their use is likely to spread into school and across the age range. They represent an attempt to move away from norm–referencing into a methodology which attempts to record what the child can do in a positive way. Humanities departments should employ those assessment techniques which seem appropriate. They should use behavioural techniques where suitable and begin to develop strategies for a levels of response approach where these are misplaced.

Where level of response schemes are used, it is important that teachers should realise that the descriptions which they design for particular pieces of work to represent different levels of response, apply to those pieces of work solely, and not to the child. It is not the intention that a child should become labelled as a level C child. The function of teachers is to try to teach children to reach the higher level not simply to accept the level they initially achieve as being where they will end up. There is a danger that children who initially achieve only at a low level will be expected to stay at that level. There is some research describing how students can be encouraged to improve their responses and reach higher levels of judgement by structured programmes of teaching. Many of these programmes involve questions which challenge the students' responses and seek to improve the quality of their thinking. For example:

> *Statement:* In the Middle Ages most men lived all their lives without being able to read. They built beautiful cathedrals but did not know many of the ordinary, everyday things which every child of twelve knows nowadays. Every age builds upon the knowledge of those who went before. *Question:* Were the people of the Middle Ages clever or stupid? How do you know?

Among the many teaching questions which sought to encourage the students to consider more deeply the question, were these.

(a)   Does it say that all men of the Middle Ages were unable to read?
(b)   Are you always clever because you can read?
(c)   Is a person who cannot read always stupid?
(d)   Are all people clever nowadays?
(e)   Why is it that many ordinary modern children of twelve know more about some things than very clever people of the past?
(Peel, 1971, p. 121)

Use of this sort of structured questions had the effect, in this study, of raising the students' level of response, in some cases considerably. Teachers will see the possible applications that this type of approach has for other humanities subjects which use levels of response marking.

At a time when teachers are expected to bear a larger burden of assessment it is crucially important both in examination classes and in those for younger children that teachers do not become blinded to the fact that they are teachers. They are assessors in so far as it assists in the teaching process and aids the evaluation of their own work. They should not lose an opportunity to teach simply because they are also assessing. With the concentration on school-based assessment in the GCSE, especially in coursework, there is a danger of this: that teaching opportunities will be lost because the primary concern of some lessons is assessment.

TEACHING CONCEPTS

As has been pointed out above, much of the work done in humanities departments is conceptual in nature. One of the most important reasons for studying humanities subjects is that they may provide the child with valuable conceptual understanding. Unfortunately, children with learning difficulties are too often exposed to concepts without actually being taught to understand them. Possibly this is due, in part, to the prevalence of Piagetian thought in English education. There is a popular myth that concepts cannot be taught to certain adolescent children because they have not reached the particular level of thinking which Piaget had set down as being that necessary for concept formation – formal operational thought. This is in fact a misunderstanding of neo-Piagetian thought. The conditions for cognitive development which he specifies have been applied to advantage and to the education of adolescents with learning difficulties by Feuerstein with his theories of cognitive modifiability and Instrumental Enrichment.

Practically this misunderstanding seems to have meant that humanities teachers have shied away from complex concepts in the belief that their children cannot learn them. This is unfortunate. Not only can concepts be taught but, if there is to be any point in teaching humanities to children with learning difficulties, they must be. However, there is no point in merely exposing these children to concepts and hoping that, by magic, they will be understood. They must be taught. In secondary schools, as most are still organised, not enough time is given to individual subject areas for the teacher to elucidate the message through the medium. If there is a week between individual lessons, it is asking too much to expect the child with learning difficulties to remember both the content and the concept implicit in that content. The concept must be made explicit.

If humanities teachers have discovered that children with learning difficulties have struggled with concepts they should consider whether they actually tried to teach the concept, or obscured it in a contextual framework. Teachers have to make plain to these children what the concept under discussion is and seek to illustrate this generalisation by many concrete examples. The content is easily forgotten, but the concept can remain, and of the two the concept is far more important for, by definition, its nature gives it applicability in many situations.

To give an example, traditionally, teachers who were teaching a course in modern world history would teach the rise to power of Stalin, Mussolini and Hitler and apply themselves to the character of their regimes, since these were on the syllabus. It may be true that for the future study of history it is important to know the intricacies of all three regimes; it may be true that all three regimes are intrinsically interesting and fascinating areas of study. It cannot, however, be true that a knowledge of them is vital to the existence of most children after they leave school. A much stronger case can be advanced that people leaving school should have some idea of what a 'dictatorship' is. If this is the case then time which previously might have been spent on the suppression of the Kulaks should more properly be spent on teaching of an important concept – dictatorship. If by doing this we reduce the historical content and if the definition of 'dictatorship' is incomplete, the activity can still be justified in terms of the four Rs (see above). The humanities department has to consider the essential issue. If it does not take responsibility for the teaching of concepts of this type then where else on the school curriculum will children have an opportunity to learn them? They will come across them out of school, in newspapers and on television and the danger is that they will apply incomplete or erroneous definitions to the words they read or hear.

Instead of allowing children who have difficulties to plod through the march on Rome or be consumed by the Reichstag fire, the history teacher now has the task of reducing the concept of 'dictatorship' to its barest essentials. A checklist, see Figure 4.4, is prepared which might try to teach the concept by contrasting it with democracy. When each of the component parts of the common characteristics which make up the concept 'dictatorship' and the concept 'democracy' has been listed and explained by examples, the child can then look through the information on Hitler, Stalin and Mussolini. This section of the study, through using adapted and modified materials will, nevertheless, explore questions of evidence and much the same content and skills as previously. The difference is that there is a structure to the study which exists as a point of reference. By judicious use of the checklist the child, even

	YES	NO
Free parliament		
Free elections		
Freedom of speech		
Freedom of belief		
Freedom of assembly		
Freedom to form trade unions		
Freedom from arrest without trial		
Free courts		

Figure 4.4 Democracy and dictatorship

those with learning difficulties, can come to an understanding of the essential concepts. The 'core' of this study, therefore, is an understanding of 'democracy' and 'dictatorship'. This is what all children take away with them. Those who are unable to remember such content as they might need for the final examination have nevertheless achieved the core. They might not be aware of the Night of the Long Knives, or know its date, but they will be aware that the illegal and violent liquidation of political opponents is likely to occur in a dictatorship.

Important in classes which include both potentially high achievers and children with learning difficulties is that such an approach does not reduce the examination chances of high achievers. In fact, since it provides them, as well, with the fundamental concepts it is time well spent. It is far more efficient in terms of teaching time than to teach the three regimes and to expect some of the children to 'pick up' the concept almost accidentally. It is an ideal way to approach work in a class in which there is a great divergence of competence in history, since all with careful nurturing can gain something from the study.

Concepts taught in this way can be assessed according to the principles of objectives-based instruction and criterion–referenced assessment. A mythical or real political system can be given to the children and they can match the case study to the criteria given on the checklist. Their conclusions as to whether they are dealing with a dictatorship or a democracy tests their understanding of the concept which has been the focus of the teaching. The criterion, in this case, need not necessarily be 100 per cent accuracy, for we can argue that it is enough to know the main aspects of these differing systems of government without knowing them all. Life beyond schools requires a basic understanding in order to cope with television and newspaper reports of what is going on in the world, not a complete understanding. Schools, nevertheless, do have a responsibility to provide children with the mental framework to deepen their understanding in later life.

They will be aware, for example, that not all regimes or political systems fall into neat compartments, i.e. they are neither democracies nor dictatorships. The awareness of the complexity of politics can be an objective in itself. Not all children have to understand all these complexities.

This conceptual approach is well suited also to the demands of modern geography teaching with its emphasis on conceptual understanding and the ability to use learned generalisations. It is the easiest and most effective way to reach these objectives. An important concept, usually introduced quite early in the secondary school is that of settlement. Children need to know what a settlement is and to apply the generalised principle to a whole variety of case studies. Using the checklist approach again, teachers would analyse the nature of 'settlement'. The results of this analysis would be presented on a checklist, see Figure 4.5, which the children would apply to a series of situations. In this way the 'rule' would be induced and then applied. Unlike the example from history given above, this would probably represent no more than one lesson's teaching.

	LIVED IN	MANY PEOPLE TOGETHER	PERMANENT
Village			
City			
Farm			
Caravan site			
Army barracks			
Airport			
School			
Supermarket			
Town			

Figure 4.5   Settlement

The time spent in making sure that the children understood the various terms used would clearly depend on their pre-skills, i.e. what they understand already. Moreover teacher help would also depend on how quickly the children grasped the ideas involved. Since it uses a checklist approach the learning of the concept can be assessed by criterion–referencing. The test would consist of further examples. For children with learning difficulties some of the same examples would be given to increase confidence and new examples would be fully explained. In this list, for example, some children would not understand what an army barracks was. This would need to be explained to ensure that this lack of understanding did not become a cause of failure. The criterion would be to demonstrate 100 per cent accuracy. Anything less than 100 per cent would be unsatisfactory since it would denote a lack of understanding of one of the points necessary for an understanding of the concept. By using the child's responses and by questioning, it is an easy task to discover the point and cause of failure and remove it.

A final example demonstrates how, with careful handling, a group of concepts can be taught. If we consider this question from history:

What conditions were necessary for an Industrial Revolution to occur in Britain? How were these conditions satisfied?

we would probably agree that it is not the kind of question which is suitable to address with a group of children with learning difficulties. The traditional view would be that there are too many concepts and not enough concrete material involved for children in this population to have any chance of success. However, with careful planning such students are able to master the essential ideas.

Again, the initial task is to consider the teaching points to be made. What is it that the teacher wishes the children to learn from the course of study? In terms of concepts it is useful to consider what they might need after school, i.e. what is real? There might be general agreement in a department that it would be useful if children knew and understood what 'things' were necessary for any business to begin. Rather than instruct the children in this from the outset, a teacher might decide to let them come to the realisation themselves. So the first lesson which dealt with the topic might start with the words: 'What you are going to learn today is what you need to start a business. This is likely to be important for some of you after you leave school, or even before that if you've seen what the fourth years are doing in their mini-enterprise scheme ... ' This sets the objective in the minds of the children and gives them a long-term and a shorter-term justification for reaching it.

The children would then be split into groups, carefully arranged to give a spread of ability (clearly even in a class which includes many children with learning difficulty some will have more competence than others). The task of each group would be to list all the things it might need in order to start a business making a particular item (anything which some of the class appeared to be interested in). It is surprising how good children are at this exercise. We normally do these lessons with third year pupils and they usually have little difficulty in working out through discussion and some prompting that:

1. Businesses exist to make things to sell to people to make profit for the people who began the business.
2. Money is needed to start the business off.
3. People are needed to do the work.
4. Machinery may be needed to make the goods.
5. Power is needed to drive the machines.
6. 'Things' are needed to work on to make the final goods.
7. People are needed to buy the things when they are made. (Many groups omit this initially but a gentle nudge soon makes the point obvious to them.)

The teacher then translates their group work into the language of economics. The children generally enjoy this if it is explained that this is the language which adults in business use. From their list, then, they eventually arrive at an understanding that business requires

Capital
Labour
Plant (machinery)
Power
Raw materials
Markets.

Once this is established it is a fairly easy job using primary and secondary sources, presented at an appropriate level, to overlay the historical content of the early industrialisation on to this framework, provided that previous lessons have given the group the background knowledge they need. For example, if the idea of many people moving from the countryside into the towns looking for work after the Agricultural Revolution has been fully explored, it is usually easy for the children to appreciate that these people could find work in the new factories.

The important point is that even if the content concerning early industrialisation is forgotten, the essential principles of how to start a business remain. The conceptual understanding of this will remain with children with learning difficulties long after John Kay's Flying Shuttle has disappeared.

LEARNING TO LEARN

Almost by definition children who have learning difficulties need tuition in how best to learn. How these students can be taught to cope with various sorts of material is the subject of Chapter 6. This short section deals essentially with study skills. Humanities departments need to have reference skills among their stated objectives. Children need to be confident about finding information. They need to understand, for example, how to use a contents and an index and they need to be shown where things are in the library. The teaching of these sorts of skills cannot be left to other departments. In addition, humanities teachers need to assist children with learning difficulties to learn in school and at home so that their learning may, eventually, become more independent.

In the last fifteen years some work has been done on study skills or revision skills and presented in appropriate formats for students. Much of this material, however, usually appears in secondary schools – in those schools where it appears at all – as part of a package which is used during form period or in lessons of personal and social education. We believe that such material should be introduced 'across the curriculum'. There is no conclusive evidence that children do transfer skills across the curriculum unless the school as a whole stresses particular policies in all subject areas. Children with learning difficulties require some training in study skills in their humanities lessons as they do in other curricular areas.

Our experience suggests that children are fascinated by the basic points involved in the psychology of memory. They enjoy the teacher sharing with them the rationale of going over something which they did last week or a month ago, 'to make sure it sticks'. They are generally interested to know how they can improve their powers of recall.

There are ample sources of material for teachers to use in considering how to present the issues of learning to learn to children with learning difficulties. There are useful hints in *Active Tutorial Work* (Hamblin, 1979), for example. Humanities teachers are not advised to take lesson plans from programmes of this type and present them in humanities time, but to use the main points and reinforce them when the time seems appropriate.

Simply, some of the main points which children need to know are these:

- Things which have been learned are soon forgotten unless you remind yourself of them. It is therefore important to look over things which were learned last week at least for four weeks. Then you can afford to look at them less often.
- When trying to learn things you have already understood try to work out ways of thinking about what you are trying to learn that will help you (e.g. acronyms, cartoons or other mnemonics; teachers will need to give plenty of assistance in designing these).
- If you are working at home, try to work where you have:
  a strong light directing your eyes onto the work;
  as much quiet as possible, unless you want to work with music which for some people is better;
  at a table or a desk, if possible, and on an upright chair: armchairs often make you go to sleep.
- Make sure:
  you split up the time into short periods and relax every so often. (For children with learning difficulties whose attention span may be short, it is sensible to cut the recommended times, which frequently are half an hour with a five-minute break at the end. These students might be better with quarter of an hour and a ten-minute break);
  you find someone who will test you to see if you know it. (This can be a useful starting point for schools to enlist the co-operation of parents.)

This advice can be of tremendous value to a child with learning difficulties as well as being of great value to higher achievers. The process needs to start in the first year (if not in the primary school). There is little point in leaving such advice until fourth year exams approach when many children with learning difficulties may have lost the inclination to learn. By that stage study skills may be a profound irrelevance to them.

To reduce this possibility and to achieve the objectives which humanities departments set themselves and their students, careful thought needs to be given to the organisation of the department and the classroom. Equal consideration needs to be given to the human and material resources which the department may deploy. Chapters 5 and 6 address these crucial issues.

REFERENCES

Ainscow, M. and Muncey, J. (1981) *Small Steps: A Workshop Guide about Teaching Children with Learning Difficulties*. Coventry LEA.

Ainscow, M. and Muncey, J. (1987) *Special Needs in the Secondary School* (Special Needs Action Project). Cardiff: Drake.

Black, H. D. and Goring, R. (1983) *A Diagnostic Resource in Geography.* Edinburgh: Scottish Council for Research in Education.

Bloom, B. S. (1956) *Taxonomy of Educational Objectives Handbook One: Cognitive Domain.* New York: McGraw-Hill.

Boardman, D. (1986) 'Planning with objectives'. In Boardman, D. (ed.) *Handbook for Geography Teachers.* Sheffield: The Geographical Association.

Brennan, W. K. (1979) *Curricular Needs of Slow Learners.* Schools Council Working Paper 63. London: Evans/Methuen Educational.

Bruner, J. (1960) *The Process of Education.* Harvard University Press.

Coltham, J. and Fines, J. (1971) *Educational Objectives for the Study of History.* London: The Historical Association.

Dilkes, J. (1982) 'The weather with remedial groups'. In Boardman, D. (ed.) *Geography with Slow Learners.* Sheffield: The Geographical Association.

Gard, A. and Lee, P. J. (1978) '"Educational Objectives for the Study of History" reconsidered'. In Dickenson, A. K. and Lee, P. J. (eds) *History Teaching and Historical Understanding.* London: Heinemann.

Gulliford, R. (1979) 'Remedial work across the curriculum'. In Gains, C. W. and McNicholas, J. A. (eds) *Remedial Education: Guidelines for the Future.* London: Longmans.

Hamblin, B. (1979) *Active Tutorial Work.* Lancashire LEA.

Mager, R. F. (1962) *Preparing Instructional Objectives.* Belmon, Ca: Frearon.

McCall, C. (1982) 'Some national reports and surveys: implications for the remedial specialist'. In Hinson, M. and Hughes, M. (eds) *Planning Effective Progress.* Amersham: Hulton Educational.

Muncey, J. and Ainscow, M. (1983) Launching SNAP in Coventry. *Special Education: Forward Trends,* **10**, 3.

Nichol, J. (1981) *What Is History?* Oxford: Basil Blackwell.

Northern Examining Association (1985) *GCSE: History – Syllabus 'B'.* London: HMSO.

Peel, E. A. (1971) *The Nature of Adolescent Judgement.* London: Granada.

Rollins, G. (1985) 'Social skills and personal development'. In Corney, G. and Rawling, E. (eds) *Teaching Slow Learners through Geography.* Sheffield: The Geographical Association.

Scottish Council for Research in Education (1984) *Criterion Referenced Assessment in the Classroom.* Edinburgh: SCRE.

Secondary Education Council and the Open University (1984) *GCSE Teachers Guide for History.* London: HMSO.

Wilson, M. D. (1985) *History for Children with Learning Difficulties.* London: Hodder and Stoughton.

—5—

Organisation, teachers, language and communication

ORGANISATION

Much recent work has highlighted the importance of a whole-school approach to special needs. We do not wish to rehearse these issues but to apply them to the humanities department and the teachers within it. Teachers of humanities, like everyone else, have to work within the constraints of the educational establishment in which they work. Schools have developed their own organisational strategies and are at different stages of development. In some schools, for example, there may be a whole-school approach to handwriting development or to spelling development which individual teachers must take into account in the planning of their own lessons. In some the rôle of the special needs department may be well defined in terms of cross-curricular support. In others, special needs will still be met in terms of a traditional remedial department, although its name may have changed. Teachers need to have an overview of what is going on in their schools if they are to be effective teachers of children with learning difficulties. Teachers need to understand and use:

1. The whole-school policy;
2. The departmental policy;
3. The classroom policy.

Figure 5.1 shows a possible model for teachers who wish to analyse their own situation. While heads of department might have a major contribution to make with respect to a whole-school policy in their forum within the school, we are more interested in departmental policy and classroom policy. It is outside the scope of this book to deal with the development of whole-school policies. More important for humanities teachers is what happens in their lessons and in their departments. Collectively, teachers in a department may use the ideas on curriculum design, assessment, and objectives for children with learning difficulties to formulate a departmental policy for humanities learning. This should determine the practice found in the classroom context.

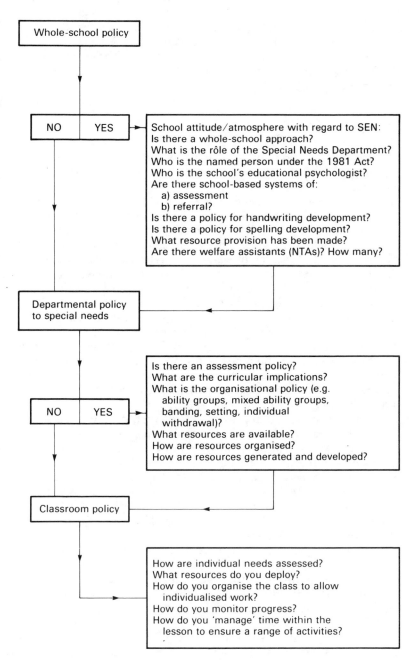

Figure 5.1

Our concentration in this and the next chapter is on the classroom situation because it is the 'point of delivery' which is most important in teaching children with learning difficulties. Those wishing to develop a departmental policy will find hints on organisation of the department along the way.

THE TEACHER

The last twenty years have seen various fashions in theories of teaching from didactic teaching to the teacher as the creator of a learning facility, from talk-and-chalk lessons through to lessons based entirely on worksheets. For all these fashions one important truth remains. The teacher is the greatest resource for learning. The relationships the pupils have in their working day are the most important factors in the success or failure of their learning experiences. The research of Galton and Wilcocks (1983) suggested that teaching style was a dominant force in the classroom. They pointed to the existence of a group they called 'easyriders' – those who dissolved into the grey unnoticed areas of the classroom, those who made few demands on teacher time and those whose career in school was more one of regression than progression. Children with learning difficulties are often to be found among this group. They are those who keep their heads down sufficiently to create few 'problems' but in reality are learning little. In identifying such children and in taking steps to make their experiences in school more positive the rôle of the teacher is pre-eminent.

As we have indicated in previous chapters, the knowledge which the teacher has of the subject area is crucial. Without a wide knowledge of the principles on which history, geography or other humanities subjects are based, the teacher is unable to see the essentials of those disciplines and present them in an acceptable learning package to the child. Equally, without a firm knowledge of an appropriate instructional process, the teacher is unable to make much headway with a class or an individual. In short, the teacher is vital to the learning process.

Further, the teacher is a vital part of a situation which is intensely human in its composition. The teacher is an adult amongst children, a motivator, a figure of authority, an interpreter of the world, an explainer of often complex rules within the school, an exemplar. Moreover, the teacher can be called upon to be supporter, friend, confidant(e) and even social worker. All of this holds true for teachers of humanities subjects to all children, not just those with special needs. However, the nature of the teacher is a much more important factor in the life of the child with learning difficulties.

Teachers of these children have to be special if they are to promote optimal learning in their classrooms. In many cases they have to rebuild a child's sense of worth, which many years of failure may have eroded. They have to be sensitive to the frustrations caused by an apparent inability to grasp something when everyone else has. They have to be skilled in making the classroom atmosphere one which supports and does not deny children with difficulties.

For teachers who undertake these daunting tasks we offer a checklist of questions.

Do you 'come through the glass'?
Children with learning difficulties frequently need the sort of support from their teachers which cannot be given by those who rely on an imposition of social distance between teacher and pupil. These children often respond much better to those teachers who are prepared, apparently, to allow their guard to drop to a degree where children can see that teachers, too, are human. The building of trusting and caring relationships with children who have learning difficulties is a vital part of creating an atmosphere conducive to learning. As Hanko (1985) wrote of John, the subject of a case study:

> He seemed to become 'teachable' with teachers who asserted authority firmly but not punitively, whom he could not goad into the aggressiveness which he himself felt towards authority figures and who could see in him not a boy who challenged their authority but a boy who needed their guidance into adulthood, whose 'bluff' they could call jocularly but without ridicule and whose 'reality' they appreciated
>
> (p. 37)

Do you really listen to what they have to say?
If confidence is to be established between learner and teacher then children need to feel assured that they are valued. It may be that the school as an institution places great value on academic success. This may leave children with learning difficulties wondering what there is in school for them. However, even in schools where this is so, it is possible to make particular teachers' rooms havens from the storms of achievement which echo round the rest of the building. It is possible to create an atmosphere in which learning, though slow, is seen as important and in which it can be supported. The humanities room should be one of these, simply because subjects under discussion concern human motivation. Discussion with groups and individuals should be one of the humanities teacher's aims. Seeking sensitivity towards other people separated in time or place cannot be achieved if the atmosphere in the classroom is not one based on a similar sensitivity. Humanities teachers need to keep a watchful eye

on the social dynamics of their teaching groups and be conscious of the way other children react towards those who have difficulties. This is especially true in mixed-ability classes.

Another important way in which this atmosphere can be fostered is by ensuring that the teacher really listens to what the children have to say. For many children with learning difficulties oral communication is vital: their writing may be illegible; their reading may be below a functional level. Most will have opinions and need to be given a secure environment in which to express them. The humanities department should ensure that it creates the conditions where this communication is encouraged. The prerequisite of this is for the teacher to be genuinely interested in what the children have to say.

Moreover, it is not enough simply to listen. It may be that the children have valid points which concern their lessons. They may find some topics boring. They should be encouraged to explore the reasons why this might be so. In all cases the teacher should make the attempt to explain why the particular topic is important, what skills are being acquired by the type of approach. If teachers are to show genuine respect for the children as a starting point for learning, then they must expect 'consumer participation in planning and evaluating lessons' (Smith, 1982). Further, they should encourage this. This approach may be far removed from traditional pedagogic practice. Nevertheless, it is in line with current thinking on active learning and reflects the trend towards negotiated curricula. If children with learning difficulties feel some 'ownership' of their own learning the teacher's task is eventually made easier.

Do children feel that their work is appreciated?
Praise is a vital part of teaching. Positive reinforcement is clearly a more important aid to learning for a child whose self esteem is low. High achievers can often do with less. For children with learning difficulties praise is vital. However, if the children perceive that this praise is not meant, or perceive that the work they have completed is not worthy of praise, its usefulness as a means of reward is limited. In addition, it is essential that the distribution of praise is a subtle process. Simple repetitive statements of praise wear thin very quickly. Teachers need to ensure that the way in which they give praise is varied and, in the perceptions of the children, really have the effect of positively reinforcing the behaviour. Also, as Smith (1982) has pointed out, it may, as part of a structured programme, be necessary to create simple tasks initially so that the teacher is in a position to find things to praise.

The rôle of the support teacher

Clunies-Ross's review (1985) suggests that many schools do not employ a system of support teachers. They prefer instead to pursue a more traditional model of withdrawing children with learning difficulties for basic subjects. As we have seen, however, current trends suggest that more schools will be moving towards the use of their special needs staff in the rôle of support teachers. It is an essential function of the heads of humanities departments to ensure that support teachers are not used solely for supporting learning in 'basic subjects'. Support teachers have a vital rôle to play and can provide essential flexibility in the organisation of humanities lessons whether they be with mixed ability groups or with groups specifically composed of children with learning difficulties.

The greatest problem in following structured programmes with children with learning difficulties is that they clearly will not learn at the same rate. Ideally, these children would benefit from instruction which was individualised. However, the English secondary school, in terms of resources and staff deployment, is geared to group instruction. Many of the techniques detailed in the rest of this book apply to a group instruction approach for that reason even though it is frequently an inadequate response to the needs of children with learning difficulty. Research (cf. Galton, Simon and Croll, 1980) has suggested that where teachers employ individualised instruction techniques within a group, it is extremely difficult to keep the rest of the class 'on task'. In other words, teachers experience great difficulty in maximising the learning of the whole group when working with individuals or very small groups. Teachers will recognise the scene only too well. Time spent in trying to teach one child in a class of 30 frequently is interrupted by the necessity of having to control the rest of the group. Even if the rest of the class is working quietly it is not easy to judge whether the children are actually working on assigned tasks. In addition, if the tasks on which the group is engaged are demanding and challenging there will be questions throughout the lesson. The teacher is frequently pulled in different directions, the individualised instruction is interrupted while questions are asked and answered and teaching and learning are inefficient. The danger, in short, is that the learning of the vast majority will suffer at the expense of the small group of children with learning difficulties who are receiving much closer attention and that attention itself will fall short of what was intended.

Teachers need to be sensitive to the strengths and weaknesses of each group. Some will more easily accept these periods of working with a teacher in the room who is not directly supervising their learning. With others such an approach will be impossible. However, a whole range of possibilities open up if a support teacher can be provided.

There is an increasing volume of literature on the rôle of the support teacher as those previously involved in 'remedial' education seek a re-definition of their rôles. The support teacher is seen as a consultant who comes from the special needs department and provides help and advice as often for teachers as for children (Hart, 1986; Hallmark, 1983; Garnett, 1983). Hanko (1985) has suggested that such support teachers need to promote 'coping strategies' for teachers as the emphasis moves away from the problems of pupils to the instructional process. The good support teacher is seen as a fellow professional who will provide help, as Bines (1986) suggests, without stigma. The theory behind this redefinition is clear. Simply, if effective communication can be facilitated between the subject teacher and the support teacher gains can be made which are more easily maintained even when help is withdrawn (Thomas, 1986).

For teachers in humanities departments such additional help would be welcomed, but it cannot be taken for granted. It is as likely that the 'extra' teacher in a particular class will come from other backgrounds as it is that they will be trained specifically in special needs. The support teacher who comes from the special needs department may bring several benefits which other in-class support teachers cannot. For example, if the special needs department has responsibility for co-ordinating cross-curricular knowledge about individual children, support teachers who have their base there are more likely to be in a position to point out that a particular child will not be able to cope with a particular lesson in geography. Knowledge of a child's progress or difficulties in the maths lesson may lead a support teacher to suggest in advance that a geography lesson on scale will be beyond the child since that child does not have the necessary pre-skills in measurement with a ruler to get much from the lesson. Alternative strategies could therefore be worked out in advance. However, there is no guarantee that a special needs support teacher will be available for that particular class. As Galloway (1985) pointed out, who receives what help often depends on administrative factors. The constraints placed on staff deployment by the timetable in the secondary school frequently dictate whether Ms X or Mr Y receive extra support with 3S on Friday afternoon, and certainly whether such help comes from someone who is trained in special needs. It is clearly quite impossible for a special needs department to provide the assistance required by all pupils with learning difficulties in every department for all of the week.

In a search for an appropriate strategy across the whole school some institutions have experimented with different models. Giles and Dunlop (1986) describe a scheme in which subject teachers developed their professional expertise by working as support teachers at various times of the week. They describe the allocation of these teachers to classrooms according to pupil need and their own preference; interestingly most of the support teachers in the study chose to work away from their own subject area. Thomas and Jackson (1986) describe another scheme in which each department within the school nominated a key co-ordinator. These 'key' teachers were involved in all stages from planning to implementing a whole-school policy to meet special needs while retaining their membership of the departmental team.

These strategies seem likely to be the forerunner of other schemes in which subject teachers assist colleagues with classes in which children with special needs have been identified. The classroom humanities teacher cannot be guaranteed the assistance of another teacher. However, no offer of help should be spurned. Equally the head of department should actively seek the assistance of another teacher with classes which contain children with learning difficulties.

There are, however, several ground rules which need to be set in the use of the teacher who supports children in another's lesson. The area is fraught with difficulty.

1. Discussion must take place between class teacher and support teacher before each lesson. Bines' research (1986) suggests that many support teachers arrive in a lesson without being aware of the objectives of that lesson, its content, or the skills and attitudes that the teacher wishes to draw out. It is important, therefore, that the support teacher has read and discussed the curriculum document of the department concerned and is aware of the long-term goals of the department. This is likely to take some time, especially if the support teacher is not a humanities specialist. It is important that the support teacher has read and assimilated the particular scheme of work which is being used. Discussions and joint planning should take place between the classroom teacher and the support teacher before each lesson. If these essential steps are not taken, there is a danger that the rôle of the support teacher becomes nothing more than 'riding shotgun' for the class teacher who is 'doing the lesson'. The rôle deteriorates into that which dictates that the chief purpose is to keep 'difficult' children quiet so that the teacher can teach. Arguably, some of this

kind of work is inevitable, but it should not be the chief purpose.

2. Class teacher and support teacher need to establish mutual trust. This can be a traumatic process. Many teachers still do not welcome other adults into their classrooms; many become defensive when faced with a situation in which their work can be judged by their peers. Heads of humanities departments should try to encourage an open classroom policy and should attempt to organise an atmosphere based on support and not judgement. This may be increasingly difficult as the formal appraisal of teachers receives a higher profile in schools. Nevertheless, teachers working together as class and support teachers need to feel that their performance will not be judged by the other, and certainly not be discussed with others outside that classroom behind their backs. To a certain extent support teachers who come from the special needs department are better placed to establish this trust for they will perform a similar rôle across the curriculum.

3. Class teacher and support teachers need to identify appropriate strategies which will govern their actions in the classroom. While it is subject teachers' responsibility to organise the resources within their own room it is important that a parity of esteem is established in the minds of the children so that neither the subject teacher nor the support teacher is seen as superfluous. An early opportunity, for example, should be sought which gives the support teacher the task of addressing the class and performing some group instruction while the subject teacher works with some individuals. It is important that the children do not see the support teacher as the 'spare' teacher who helps the 'proper teacher' but as another, and equally important, resource in their humanities lesson. If the support teacher is always the one who works with children individually or in small groups there is likely to be a problem of status. In addition if support teachers always head straight for the target child or children at the start of each lesson, as much stigma for that child or children can result as if they had been withdrawn from that classroom for 'remedial' help. Strategies for overcoming these pitfalls include the possibility of the spport teacher taking the lead lesson and the class teacher working with groups – not necessarily the lowest achievers.

4. Class teachers and support teachers need to plan who does what in each lesson. Ideas on room management need to be discussed. There are useful models available when trying to

balance individualised teaching and class or group activity. This approach to management has been successfully used in schools for children with severe learning difficulties where, traditionally, more than one adult works in a classroom (cf. *Education and the Developmentally Young Project*, McBrien and Weightman, 1980). This room management system outlines three rôles within the classroom – an individual helper, a 'manager' who focuses the body of the class towards 'on task' activities, and a 'mover' who ensures that there is flow during the session. Thomas and Jackson (1986) suggest that a room management approach may help to define rôles where there is more than one person working in a mainstream classroom. Thomas (1985) has documented the success of one such project with primary aged children in a mainstream class. In practice mainstream classroom teachers in secondary schools may dispense with the 'mover' and concentrate on the other two rôles since the mover's rôle is essentially 'trouble shooting' (e.g. dealing with fits, accidents, etc.) which might be expected to be needed less frequently in the mainstream classroom than in a class for children with severe learning difficulties. Essentially, one teacher's rôle might be to teach small groups or individuals without interruption so that intensive instruction may occur; the other's is to ensure that the main group of children within the class are kept working and to answer their questions.

In summary, it is essential that the support teacher's rôle is clearly defined and areas of responsibility taken. If this is not achieved the effect can be a dilution of expertise and a source of animosity between teachers resulting in poor learning outcomes for the pupil. A fuller discussion of these points can be found in Thomas and Jackson's work.

Example 5.1

This lesson was observed in a mainstream secondary school of second year pupils. The year followed an integrated humanities course. The department had been used to team teaching and recently it had acquired a support teacher for these lessons to assist the learning of children with difficulties. The whole year was timetabled for humanities at the same time using four humanities teachers for the four classes. They were taught in adjoining rooms allowing some flexibility of approach. The children who had difficulty in reading 'standard' material had been placed with two teachers and it was in these teachers' room that the support teacher usually worked.

The lesson outlined below was the 'lead lesson' of a course which introduced religious difference. The course aims were heavily concerned with attitudes and a strong multicultural element underpinned all lesson plans.

At the start of the lesson the children from the four groups were ushered into their year base by the support teacher who settled them down. The four humanities teachers then entered. They had dressed up for the lesson. One dressed as a Red Indian chief, one as a Nun, one as a Buddhist and one as a learned academic. There was considerable interest among the children but little laughter as this kind of lesson was not unfamiliar to them. The support teacher then explained who the other teachers represented and that they had arrived to give their own account of 'How the world began'. Each of the 'actors' stated his or her view of this. The support teacher then invited members of the class to ask questions of the 'actors' to clarify their accounts.

At the end of the questions the two classes separated into their different rooms. With the experience fresh in their minds the children discussed the main points and others as a group. They were all encouraged to express an opinion as to which account they preferred and to try to justify their reasons. Each pupil had shared the 'concrete' experience on which to draw, even if they had never before had the opportunity to discuss religious matters. The classes shared their views and opinions. Those who had not formalised any view had the opportunity to listen to those of the others. They then broke up into smaller groups which enabled them to discuss the matter in their own and less formal language and to do some written follow up work.

It was only at this stage that the support teacher 'slipped' into the groups which contained children with learning difficulties. She helped to 'structure' the discussion to help those children to express their views. She fulfilled a number of important tasks:

1. She was able to ensure that they had understood the main points which the interviewing had been intended to bring out.

2. She was able to ensure that the written material was intelligible to all the pupils. In advance of the lesson, at the planning stage, she had consulted with the subject teachers in the department and had adapted some of their printed material so that its reading demands were lessened. Those who found the 'standard' material too demanding were provided with a simplified version, but one which did not lose the sense and essential ideas of the standard material (see Chapter 6).

This well organised, well planned, visually and intellectually stimulating lesson was well received by the children, not least by those who had learning difficulties. It was an excellent example of one method of utilising support teaching assistance. The support teacher had been involved at the planning stage. The humanities department had designed the second year curriculum and had written schemes of work for it. In this process there had, understandably, been no input from the support teacher. However, from the moment when the humanities department decided what it wanted to teach, the support teacher was involved. She knew what the objectives of the lesson were. She was seen deliberately by the children as an important and equal member of the humanities team by sorting out the classes at the start of the lesson and by acting as chair of the interviews. She had adapted materials so that they were entirely suitable to the children she was going to teach in a small group and had performed the essential function of the special needs or support teacher – she had accessed the mainstream curriculum to children with learning difficulties.

Non-teaching assistants

There is a growing number of non-teaching assistants, especially in those areas of the country where children are given additional hours help if they are the subject of a Statement under the 1981 act. Quite clearly the rôle of the NTA is different to that of a teacher and teachers should be careful not to misuse NTAs by deploying them as teachers. Nevertheless, as adults who frequently have contact with children in classrooms, it is important that teachers make NTAs aware of the teaching methods followed and the objectives of particular lessons and courses. It is our experience that, far from regarding such explanations as an unwanted intrusion, NTAs are pleased to share the educational philosophy of the course and feel much more part of an adult team when they are invited to share underlying principles and particular strategies with individual children.

Situations need to be created in which welfare assistants can be free to say that a group of pupils with whom they were working were not coping with the work they had been set or that the work was too easy. Welfare assistants are in an ideal position to judge success or failure of an agreed objective provided that they are aware of the criteria of assessment. If NTAs have been given a stated task to do with a group they are in a better position to evaluate the learning outcomes that they witness. They can be used as an integral part of the assessment process and help in highlighting those approaches that do and do not help a pupil learn. Perceptions of educational thinking, when shared, can lead to positive learning outcomes for the pupils. The most effective way of sharing is through dialogue and opportunities should be created to allow this dialogue to take place. We are not suggesting that this should be an arduous or a threatening procedure, only that it should happen. Initially it will take time and thought, but as everyone involved becomes clear about the task in hand, the agreed way of working and their individual rôle within the classroom the more economical the process will become. Eventually, the dividends will far outweigh the time invested.

Parents

There is increasing interest in the rôle of parents in the education of children with special needs. We do not propose to review this as it more properly falls into studies of 'whole-school strategies' for special needs. However, humanities departments can involve parents of children with learning difficulties in their children's education in a more meaningful way than through a once or twice yearly school report and parents' evening. If the department adopts a modular approach to its work, based on school-centred profiles as records of achievement in the early years of secondary schools, the children will have something from the humanities department to take home regularly itemising progress.

Equally, much humanities work, especially in the early secondary years, can involve family history, family religious belief or family political activity. Concepts such as 'trade unionism' can be more easily understood if there is a family story to illustrate some aspect of being a member of a trade union. The child's home background may provide a particular perspective on more issues and therefore gives the opportunity for meaningful discussion.

However, humanities teachers should be careful and sensitive in the tasks they set to be done at home. It is best to set tasks for involving parental help that relate to personal experiences or beliefs, for example a family tree, which gives all the pupils the opportunity to come up with some answers. The alternative is often to highlight the differences between children and their back-grounds. An 11-year-old girl was recently observed to become quite distressed when her best friend was given credit for finding the answer to an obscure question.

'But,' she protested, 'my Mum didn't know the answer to that question.'

The teacher, trying to support the mother, replied: 'Well you should have looked it up in a book.'

'We haven't got any, Miss.' ...

There is scope for parents to be involved in humanities work, and they can be an excellent resource for learning. Ill-considered tasks, however, can often be counter-productive.

LANGUAGE

Teacher talk

'When they heard the words from the pulpit they said they were good words and very good words wondrous words, but what they were they cannot tell.' (Comment on church sermons delivered in Latin to an English congregation: Bishop Gardiner, *c.* 1540.)

'The teacher just goes on and on. He explains all the long words but we don't understand. Then he goes on at us because we don't know what we're supposed to be doing.' (12-year-old girl: 1987.)

Teachers like to talk but the language which they use when addressing the class frequently is not understood. Teacher talk is inevitable and desirable. It can convey a sense of excitement and is a crucial motivating force in the classroom. History teachers, especially, need to develop an interesting narrative style, particularly with younger secondary children for whom a powerful 'story line' is important. However, all humanities teachers need to be careful about choice of words when they are addressing their classes. This is obviously true for classes which contain children with learning difficulties. The assumptions that teachers make about the level of comprehension of the spoken words which their pupils have are often wildly inaccurate. Much of what goes on in a classroom is lost to pupils with special needs because they simply do not understand what is being asked of them. A list of expected outcomes offered to the highest achievers in a mixed-ability class can be so incomprehensible to children with learning difficulties that they switch off and become disaffected before they have begun.

Research suggests that teachers are much more conscious of the difficulties which their specialist vocabulary contains than they are of their non-specialist language and their sentence construction. History teachers would, for example, pay particular attention to the way they introduce such terms as 'agrarian', 'capitalism' or *'coup d'état'* but they might still couch their explanations in terms which would not be understood by pupils with learning difficulties in their class, or even pupils who apparently had no difficulties. One of the present authors remembers a first-year sixth form student who was attempting her history 'O' level for the third time. She talked intelligently and gave few indications of having difficulties. Her essay on the Spanish Civil War was perfectly adequate for 'O' level purposes. It was only by chance that the discovery was made that she did not actually know what a civil war was. She had either missed the explanation or simply had not understood it, but had been able to disguise her lack of comprehension for 3 years.

The following is an attempt to give helpful hints for humanities teachers wishing to raise the level of pupil comprehension in the classroom.

1. Language should be clear and simple. Complex sentences and conjunctions should be avoided. It is important to use short sentences, free from syntactical complexity and in which the use of negatives is avoided where possible: it is very easy for the 'not' not to be heard and turn the negative into a positive.

2. Short words should be used wherever possible. Where larger words are essential vocabulary, teachers should ensure that these are fully explained. Synonyms should be provided wherever possible. Explanations in the 'restricted code' of the children should be provided in the normal course of all lessons. The elaborated code of the middle-class teacher may be, for many children with difficulties, like learning a foreign language in itself. It's hard enough to comprehend the nature of 'relative location' or 'bias in written historical sources' without having these explained in a foreign language. In certain areas pronunciation may have to change in the classroom to facilitate the communication which the teacher seeks. This is not to suggest that teachers should teach only in a language which the children themselves use at break and lunchtime, but that a more adult style of speaking should be interpreted wherever appropriate so that explanations are not missed.

3. Teachers are advised to list, in advance of the lesson, those words which they want the children to know and understand. Then they need to create opportunities to teach them and to determine whether the pupils understand what they mean, whether they can read them and whether they can use them appropriately. The humanities department has a specific responsibility to extend pupils' use of language and vocabulary. Teachers, as Hull (1978) pointed out: ... *should offer special needs children success by giving them English with which they can cope and throw in more difficult, stretching materials, not incidentally and by accident, but as a result of a conscious decision ...* (p. 33) (our italic).

4. One technique which seems to reinforce vocabulary which has been acquired during a course of study is that which uses wall space intelligently. In addition to children's work and

supporting visual material, it is useful to stick the key words which have been learned onto the classroom walls, being careful to build up lesson by lesson this vocabulary. Each word, or specialist term, should be large enough to be seen by children from anywhere in the room, perhaps by using large stencils. The letters should be lower case not capitals. Experience and research demonstrates that poor readers find lower case lettering much easier to read than capitals.

Example 5.2
One teacher, we observed, had used this technique with a lower secondary history class. He had identified several key words that he wanted the children to know in connection with a unit of study on the nature of history and historical evidence. By the end of the six-week unit, along with the children's work and pictures connected with the study the wall was plastered with these key words:

evidence archives archaeology artefact primary secondary bias

At the start of each lesson the teacher spent a few moments reinforcing the learning of these words and checking that they had not been forgotten during the week. When the unit of work had been completed the words were left on the wall as a reminder to the class throughout the school year. Even when the unit was finished the teacher continued, whenever appropriate, to refer to them.

5. Teachers should monitor carefully the degree of teacher talk which occurs in their lessons. There is a danger that teacher talk takes a disproportionate amount of lesson time. It is useful from time to time to tape record a lesson. Many lessons can be learned from such an enterprise, but, as a starting point, it is useful to analyse how much teacher talk there is. In an era which encourages 'active learning' it is important to consider the relatively passive nature of listening. Pupils frequently complain of being bored by excessive teacher talk. It is not possible to lay down precise guidelines as to what constitutes a sensible proportion of the lesson to engage in teacher talk. It will depend on the subject. Some topics will require more explanation than others. It will depend on the group; some groups will require a great deal of teacher direction, while the learning of others will be much better served by little teacher talk. The time of day will also be a

crucial factor. Taking a class last lesson on Friday is usually an entirely different proposition to taking the same class first lesson on Monday morning. The class is likely to tolerate less teacher talk on the Friday than on the Monday.

However, as a general rule, teachers should guard against allowing their natural enthusiasm for their subject to 'overload' the pupils with more than they can handle in one lesson. It is more important for the teacher to set up a dialogue with pupils which encourages them to develop their thinking skills and develop their capacity for reasoning and judgement. Pupils should be assisted to recognise questions and formulate answers.

Questions

Teacher questions are an important aspect of most lessons. They are an important means to extending and developing pupils' thinking and understanding. General criticisms of the ways in which teachers approach their questioning usually centre on the type of questions they use. Modern curricular theory in the humanities suggest that factual recall does not occupy the same central position it once did. Nevertheless most questions in the humanities classroom are 'what' questions. They tend to be 'closed' – permitting of only one answer. If teachers asked closed questions exclusively it would be no surprise if they develop closed and unthinking pupils. Children are adept at reading the intonation in the teacher's voice.

It is important, then, to pre-empt the one word, right or wrong answer. 'What can you see in this picture?', 'Why do you think mine owners allowed children to work in these mines?' or 'Why do some people object to nuclear power?' are the sort of questions which children with learning difficulties should be encouraged to answer. They foster good language development in giving opportunities for extended discussion. They also approach the true nature of the study of humanities subjects in demonstrating that several explanations of human behaviour are possible and all, or none may be correct.

Many children with learning difficulties will not wish to expose themselves to possible failure within the mixed-ability class. Many will remain silent and will be unwilling to risk verbal interventions in terms of answering teacher directed questions. Nevertheless, opportunities for talking should be created in groups or individually.

Pupil language

The importance of one's speaking ability cannot be overemphasised. It is an ability more natural to man than reading or writing... the importance of speaking outweighs reading and writing by a considerable margin.

(K. J. Weber, 1978)

The importance of language across the curriculum has been well rehearsed in recent years and we do not intend to develop these arguments here. However, language is the one skill that all the 'human resources' discussed above have in common. It is our primary method of communication and one that is all too often sparsely used in the secondary classroom. It is through talking that pupils are able to clarify their thinking and use language with which they feel at ease. This is especially important in the humanities because the level of abstraction required often defeats the child with learning difficulty. As Hinson (1982) points out:

> The use of language to explore an experience often reveals what can be discovered in no other way, especially to the pupil who finds the art of abstraction difficult.
>
> (p. 155)

We believe that teachers in humanities departments need to move away, as quickly as possible, from the position which states that all lessons must have a written outcome. That such an orthodoxy has become established in the past is curious in itself. Possibly it stems from the necessity to prepare children for eventual public examinations which were, and are, written in nature. Possibly its antecedents lie in the view which considered that 'good' teachers were those with silent classrooms. In humanities classrooms nothing could be further from the truth. Interpersonal and social skills are not acquired in an atmosphere of silence; co-operation is not fostered by it; the ability to see another's point of view is not developed by it; decision-making cannot be taught through it; controversial issues, an increasingly important area of humanities work, cannot be approached through it. Is it possible that silence in the classroom and children engaged on written tasks has much more to do with classroom and social control than with education?

In any case, it is not necessary to insist that children write something down to ensure that learning has taken place. This is not to suggest that teachers do not have the responsibility to develop written skills, but that this is merely one of the functions of a teacher of humanities. Teachers must admit that we often ask children to write things down as a time filler. Pupils with learning difficulties do not have time to waste on such exercises. For these pupils talking may well be a superior way of grasping the essential principles outlined in humanities lessons. It is necessary to overcome the attitude of the children themselves to discussion for they often prefer to write things down because they seem to regard this as 'real' work whereas discussion is 'doing nothing'. However, there is some experimental evidence to suggest that oral work, and thinking problems through, especially in the humanities is an essential learning medium. As Dickinson and Lee (1984) pointed out:

> A bottom band first-year class in an Essex comprehensive, presented with an exercise in which it had to decide how (as Roman governor of Britain) it would treat the new province, soon teased out the problems involved in too harsh or too 'soft' a policy on weapons, religion, taxation and so on. The children were accustomed to having to think problems through in history. ... The equivalent top-band class, without such a background, proved anxious and reluctant about the whole enterprise, asking where the right answers were to be found.
>
> (p. 153)

Talking is a vital link in the learning process, especially in those areas of the secondary curriculum in which questions do not always have right or wrong answers. As Marland (1977) suggested, 'The way into ideas, the way of making ideas truly one's own is to be able to think them through and the best way to do this for most people is to talk them through.'

REFERENCES

Bines, H. (1986) *Redefining Remedial Education*. London: Croom Helm.

Clunies-Ross, L. (1985) 'Slow learner provision in secondary schools'. In Smith, C. J. (ed.) *New Directions in Remedial Education*. Brighton: Falmer Press.

Dickinson, A.K. and Lee, P. J. (1984) 'Making sense of history'. In Dickinson, A. K., Lee, P. J. and Rogers, P. J. *Learning History*. London: Heinemann.

Galloway, D. (1985) *Schools, Pupils and Special Educational Needs*. London: Croom Helm.

Galton, M., Simon, B. and Croll, P. (1980) *Inside the Primary School*. London: Routledge & Kegan Paul.

Galton, M. and Wilcocks, J. (1983) *Moving from the Primary Classroom*. London: Routledge & Kegan Paul.

Garnett, J. (1983) 'Providing access to the mainstream curriculum in secondary schools'. In Booth, T. and Potts, P. (eds) *Integrating Special Education*. Oxford: Basil Blackwell.

Giles, C. and Dunlop, S. (1986) Changing direction at Tile Hill. *British Journal of Special Education* 13 (3) pp. 120–3.

Hallmark, N. (1983) 'A support service to the primary school'. In Booth, T. and Potts, P. (eds) *Integrating Special Education*. Oxford: Basil Blackwell.

Hanko, G. (1985) *Special Needs in Ordinary Schools*. Oxford: Basil Blackwell.

Hart, S. (1986) In-class support teaching – tackling Fish. *British Journal of Special Education* 13 (2) June.

Hinson, M. (1982) 'Language in the secondary school'. In Hinson, M. and Hughes, M. (eds) *Planning Effective Progress*. Amersham: Hulton Educational.

Hull, J. (1978) Mixed ability history – a graded worksheet approach. *Teaching History*, **22**, pp. 33–5.

Marland, M. (1977) *Language across the Curriculum*. London: Heinemann.

McBrien, J. and Weightman, J. B. (1980) The effect of room management procedures on the engagement of profoundly retarded children. *British Journal of Mental Subnormality* **26** (1) pp. 38–46.

Smith, C. J. (1982) Helping Colleagues Cope – a consultative role for the remedial teacher. *Remedial Education* **17** (2).

Thomas, G. (1985) Room management in mainstream education. *Educational Research*, **27** (3).

Thomas, G. (1986) Integrating personnel in order to integrate children. *Support for Learning*, **1** (1) February.

Thomas, G. and Jackson, B. (1986) The whole school approach to integration. *British Journal of Special Education*, **13**, (1) March.

Weber, K. J. (1978) *Yes They Can! A Practical Guide for Teaching the Adolescent Slow Learner*. Oxford: Oxford University Press.

—6—

Resources

Pupils with special educational needs require reinforcement in a wide range of situations to consolidate their learning in different circumstances until mastery has been achieved. This often requires repetition and practice so it is important to establish a range of resources and materials that are well organised and easily retrievable. In this way reinforcement can occur without learning becoming boring and laborious. Therefore, a wide variety and large number of resources are required. As Hagerty and Hill suggest: 'The production of resources for less able children is laborious. A clear idea of information to be imparted, concepts to be developed and skills to be acquired is needed at the outset' (p. 19).

Resources are only as useful as their availability. A storage and retrieval system is essential. There is no point in mislaying work under a pile of textbooks or losing the master copy of something which went well last year. This is clearly wasteful of teacher time and effort. Ideally, as we shall develop further, written resources should be stored on disks compatible with the school's computer hardware. In this way, as long as back-up disks are made, resourcing becomes a much simpler activity. Index disks can be created and, unlike paper, it is difficult to place one file on top of another on a disk. If the disk is full another has to be used. These comments on the computer as the organiser of a department's resources apply generally, not only to those especially prepared for children with special needs. However, there are several advantages in keeping resources for these on disk as we outline below.

The problem with all resources is that we become complacent about their worth. Teachers have questioned the worth of large, wordy textbooks, for children with learning difficulties. However, it is important to look critically at the range of resources which are employed – the worksheets, workcards, videos, and tape recordings. It is important to monitor the usefulness of the learning that is going on from the resources being used and assess the degree to which the resources enable the pupil to reach the stated educational goals. This should be a continuous process.

The resources we wish to consider here are written materials, both textbooks and worksheets; computers, as a resource for children as well as teachers; videos and tape recorders, both using films and as a method of providing reinforcement for rôle play or drama, and for studying the local environment.

WRITTEN MATERIAL

The reading demands on pupils entering secondary schools are great. The expectations of performance and the ability to use texts to learn is often beyond many pupils. Even where reading ages correlate with readability levels of texts pupils often do not have the skills to use text to learn. This is especially true where non-fiction and specialist materials are used. As Bullock (1975) indicated: 'Teachers need to be aware of the reading demands of their subjects and ways in which the pupil can be helped to meet them.' This is particularly true for humanities subjects where the language of the subject and the pupils' language development may be poles apart.

The content of all materials needs to be discussed with colleagues within the department in advance, as well as the way teachers intend to use it. If the content is important and much would be lost through excessive simplification then another way will have to be found to access that content to the child with learning difficulties. Solutions to this problem will become clear during the course of this chapter, but they include, putting the piece of writing on tape, having the information read by another pupil or enlisting the support of another teacher. When the material is being used in the course of a lesson it is important to check that it has been understood. This means asking questions, sitting with individuals during the lesson as they work, not assuming that because no one has asked everyone understands. All teachers will have anecdotes which illustrate the mismatch which can occur between what we assume children will know and what they actually do know.

One girl was considering her information and worksheet on the Domesday Survey. She had carried out many surveys as part of her humanities work in primary school but obviously was not clear as to what she had to write about. When the teacher specifically asked her what a survey was, she thought for a while before answering: 'I don't know.' Further discussion helped her to remember: 'We had to have a survey done before we bought our house last year. Rentokil did it.' Little wonder that her page had remained empty for most of the lesson.

The Schools Council Project 1978–82 *Reading for Learning in the Secondary School* outlined five stages of reading for learning. They are amplified in Lunzer and Gardner's work (1979).

1. Decoding;

2.　Making sense of what is said;
3.　Comparing this with what one knows already;
4.　Making judgements about the materials;
5.　Revising one's ideas.

It is the third stage which is decisive. Is the reader able to compare what is read with what is already known? When this occurs it is easy for the making of judgements and the revision of one's ideas to follow and learning to take place. This ability and willingness to reflect leads to good comprehension. Conversely, inability or unwillingness can lead to grave disadvantage for the 'poor' reader. If the reader has difficulty decoding language, has poor understanding due to limited language/vocabulary and is unable to make sense of what is said, stage 3 – the all important stage for learning to take place – becomes impossible: the written word as a resource becomes totally inappropriate to the stated teaching objective; the pupil cannot learn from the resources provided. Pupil, teacher and resource have become ineffective. If a resource is to be used, it must be effective.

Standard textbooks

There is an increasing number of textbooks which purport to cater for 'lower ability pupils' or 'slow learners'. Our task is not to give lists of books which we believe to be appropriate because our contention is that children's needs are individual and teachers need to be sensitive to them. A list of 'appropriate' materials would not necessarily meet the individual needs. Rather, our purpose is to provide suggestions as to how teachers might review books and how they might use what they already have.

Teachers should, therefore, review books carefully to see if they do suit the needs of their children. Readability (see pages 123–30) is an important issue but it is not the only one. In addition, for example, teachers should ensure that books really can fulfil the task of allowing children to reach the stated teaching objectives. It is unlikely that one text book will do this. It may be more appropriate for departments to build up a resource of many textbooks and not put their faith in one or two sets for particular groups. If for no other reason, this strategy is not to be encouraged, since children with learning difficulties need variety. Facing these children with the same textbook for each lesson will simply bore them.

However, most textbooks, including those written for high achievers, do have some applicability for children with learning difficulties provided they are used in an appropriate manner. Increasing numbers of textbooks in the humanities subjects make use of a whole variety of methods of presenting material. These include, maps, graphs, diagrams, photographs, and case studies. Children with learning difficulties should use textbooks. They need to see how these books operate, with indexes, chapters, and contents pages. It is difficult, for example, for children to develop reference skills unless they have access to at least some textbooks. This is an area in which Brennan's (1979) view that it is not essential for children with learning difficulties to understand everything with which they come into contact in school prevails (see Chapter 4). They should, therefore, know of the existence of things they fail to understand and should be encouraged to use textbooks although not in the way in which the highest achievers might. Children with learning difficulties should be directed to particular paragraphs, charts, maps, etc., in standard textbooks, without being expected to read whole chapters or sections. It is often possible for the teacher to provide a supplementary sheet with a glossary of difficult terms, or to use a paragraph in a textbook and design a cloze procedure exercise around it.

Equally, textbooks may be the best source of well produced photographs and these should be the basis of discussion and observation for children with learning difficulties. It is not necessary, always, for children to be able to read well to get something out of looking at a textbook. However, children with learning difficulties will require many other resources if they are to learn effectively (Sayer, 1987).

Worksheets

As a tool for learning, the worksheet has serious limitations. Its overuse can have a stultifying effect on the humanities curriculum, an effect which children with learning difficulties cannot afford. How many children have had their imagination slowly choked by a diet of worksheets? It is possible that if pupils are presented with nothing more than worksheets week after week, humanities lessons, which should be exciting, imaginative, and challenging, deteriorate into tedium. As a general rule, children should not arrive at their humanities lessons knowing in advance what they will be asked to do. They should be presented with a wide variety of material and a wide variety of teaching strategies. If in every lesson they come in, sit down, get out a writing book, and carry on with the worksheet they had not finished last week or start a new one, their learning experiences in humanities will be very limited. In these conditions, the 'easy-rider' flourishes; lessons become little more than time serving, doing a bit to keep 'Sir' or 'Miss' happy and waiting for the bell.

Perhaps the prevalence of a 'worksheet economy' in some departments stems from the traditional view of the 'good' teacher who runs a quiet classroom with children seated and working industriously. It is easier to control a class of children by using worksheets than in more interactive lessons. They are one of the more effective methods of classroom control, providing a focus for pupil activity and a useful means of directing children to remain 'on task'. Compared with the more fluid classroom strategies where children are required to talk as part of the learning process, worksheets are a 'safer' bet for teachers. In using games or discussion or drama as teaching strategies, there are more opportunities for things to go wrong, especially if the children are not used to working in these ways. However, a scheme of work which includes teaching method as well as aims and objectives should include a high proportion of work not based on worksheets. In any case, worksheets should always complement some other teaching strategy in the same lesson: they should never stand as the entire focus of the lesson on their own. Children, especially those who have learning difficulties need other stimulation.

Nevertheless, worksheets do have their place. Well used they can provide a valuable aid to learning. Their real value is the flexibility of activity which they allow in the classroom setting. Once a stock of graded worksheets has been developed, teachers are freed from the dilemma of what to do with whom. When teachers write worksheets which will be used by children with learning difficulties they should consider the following points, remembering, though, that they are merely guidelines:

- Does the use of language make for clear, unambiguous questions?
- Are the instructions sequenced correctly, making it absolutely clear to the children what they have to do and in what order?
- Is the vocabulary appropriately simple with simple sentence structures?
- Are the worksheets legible and clearly presented? Worksheets must be of the highest possible quality. It is not sufficient to 'run off' a hastily scribbled worksheet ten minutes before the lesson. If we expect a positive response from children it is essential to show respect for them by presenting them with well produced material. Worksheets should be typed.
- Consider the spacing and size of print. There is some debate as to the motivational nature of large type produced on a 'Jumbo' typewriter. Clearly it should be used with children who are partially sighted, with the use of relevant enlarging

technology, but for children with learning difficulties there are two possible views. Some will find it easier to read but will find it 'babyish' and insulting. Others will find it generally helpful and will not complain. As with all this advice teachers need to be sensitive to the feelings and perceptions of the particular children they teach.

- Highlight instructions and headings. Departments should establish basic rules which all members follow as to how worksheets are laid out. Many have found a team approach to worksheets and the creation of a departmental resource a valuable initiative. Consistency of approach within the department and the following of an agreed policy is a valuable aid to learning. Children will become used to the conventions of the department and will know immediately what is a main heading, what is a sub heading, what is information and what are questions. Heads of departments might raise this issue at a heads of department meeting and initiate discussions leading to a whole-school approach on worksheets. In any case, it is essential that children can tell at a glance what is a heading and what is not.

- Do not put too much information on one page. It is far more motivating for children who work slowly to finish a worksheet and know that there might be another one to do in next week's lesson, than to know that next lesson they must return and finish something off. Never finishing a task is a major problem for children with learning difficulties in mixed ability mainstream classes. Teachers should ensure that these children are able to finish something during their lessons. It is for this reason that we have great reservations about the use of 'stepped' questions on worksheets. By this, we do not mean that worksheets should not have questions which are in steps and lead towards mastery. 'Stepped' here is used in the GCSE sense i.e. the concept of having a worksheet in which the first few questions are for everyone and the later questions for higher achievers only. The theory is that the higher achievers work faster and will therefore address the more difficult questions before the end of the lesson while the lowest achiever will not even reach them. This is a recipe for frustration for the child with learning difficulties and will almost certainly lower that child's self esteem. Experience suggests that 'stepped' worksheets should be avoided.

- Offer a high ratio of picture to print. This gives a more attractive format to the worksheet. A worksheet without diagrams or pictures has little to grasp the attention of the child with learning difficulties. Also, it is important to make the pictures part of the worksheet with questions relating to them and not simply to have them there to break up the print. Much of current humanities work is concerned with the interpretation of information presented pictorially. On many worksheets, then, pictures should occupy a central position.

- Material on the worksheet should be broken up into manageable 'bites' – children then have the chance to complete a piece of work and perhaps have it marked by the teacher before starting the next section.
- Presentation has an immediate impact and should therefore be of paramount importance.

If the level of motivation is high, children will become more independent scholars, less dependent on continual teacher contact to make progress. It is important then that worksheets are not distributed to children without the ground work having been completed: A video and discussion, on which the worksheet is based, for example, will provide the context in which children with learning difficulties can make informed 'guesses' at any unknown words within the text.

When using worksheets it is important, as with all other learning tools, that children know what is required of them and why. Worksheets should therefore be relevant to the learning task. The learning steps towards the final objective where this is appropriate should have been planned in advance by the teacher and should be reflected in the worksheet. The steps should be in an ordered sequence. There should be enough small steps and there should be enough practice of each step to ensure success at the next step.

Presenting the material

There is much material within the humanities which children need to use – primary sources, maps, etc. These are often integral to a pupil's understanding of a concept. In these instances it is important that teachers find alternative ways of putting the text over to the pupil. Sometimes this is not easy. In taking an historical document the teacher can easily prepare a typed version of the text making no changes and then rewrite it into a simplified version, although, as with so much of this type of preparation, this is costly in time. Geography teachers can simplify maps although this may present more problems. There is an argument that if the originals are too simplified or the simplification is not handled sensitively, the point of using the original is lost (Allen, 1982). While there is some merit in Brennan's view (1979) that all children do not need to understand everything in school but have the right to realise the existence of things they do not understand, nevertheless this should not be regarded as an easy solution and as an excuse for not attempting alternative strategies. It is far better to provide for children who have learning difficulties material that is as simplified as much as is necessary to allow them to experience positive outcomes in their learning, and, as importantly, make them want to come again. Equally, they should be given the opportunity to look at the originals on which their simplified versions are based.

In reflective reading pupils will pause and go back to check coherence from time to time. 'Poor' readers do not do this and they need teacher intervention to help them reflect on what they have read to bring about a positive learning outcome. There are a number of strategies which can be used to increase the 'poor' reader's comprehension of written material. In essence all demand that the reader does more than read the material. For history teachers there is an excellent treatment of these methods by Cavan (1982).

Underlining

This is a technique that can be used with pupils of all abilities and is often used as a revision technique with the highest achievers. Simply, the children read the printed material and underline those parts which seem most relevant. This replaces the traditional time-consuming activity of taking notes. Many children will prefer to use a highlighting pen. As a means of ensuring that children have actually read the material this method is simple but effective and it has the advantage of concentrating the reader's mind. Its limitation is that it can only be used with duplicated material which the teacher has prepared.

Cloze

This is a common technique with which most teachers of children who are low achievers would be familiar. Simply, it involves the teacher in either writing or copying a passage from a textbook. Two or three sentences should be left untouched at the beginning of the passage. For the rest of the passage crucial words which can be worked out by context and deduced from previous teaching are deleted. Lines are added to replace the words and to create a gap. The passage needs to be well presented, preferably typed, and duplicated so that there is a copy for each pupil.

From this point, the lesson may take many forms. After a verbal introduction by the teacher the children can fill in their sheets. Alternatively, children can be divided into groups, ensuring that differing abilities in readers are in different groups. The children then work on the piece together. An important factor is that the children must be told that there may be more than one answer for each 'gap'. At a later stage in the lesson the teacher might list on the chalkboard the various answers which the children have provided and begin a class discussion.

The point of the exercise is that all the children have an incentive to read and their attention is concentrated by the necessity of filling in the gaps. Experience suggests that this is an effective way of using the printed word with children who have learning difficulties and is often an activity which is enjoyed by them. As with all strategies, however, it should not be over-used.

A further refinement is to give the children a list of possible words which might be used to fill the gaps. If this strategy is adopted the teacher should remember to avoid a unique solution. Alternatives for particular gaps should be used. The danger of unique solutions is that the children will view the answer as right or wrong when, in fact, there is a multiplicity of possible answers.

Example 6.1

This passage is taken from a 'standard' textbook. After several lessons on physical geography, the teacher gave this passage to a third year class in which there were some children with learning difficulties.

Because of the complexity of the task the words which the children had to insert were added to the bottom of the sheet.

The teacher allowed the children to discuss in small groups which words to insert before they filled in their own individual sheets.

Rivers

Rivers usually begin from _____ or bogland near the _____ of hills and moorland. They may start flowing in deep narrow channels called _____. Soon they will join other _____ to form streams. Generally these streams descend in _____ or rough, white water over waterfalls and _____.

When these streams reach lower land, they widen into rivers and flow over a _____ plain. Usually, this gets wider towards the _____ of the river. The river will wind in a series of _____. Some of these will be bypassed to leave _____ lakes. Near the sea the river may split into silty islands called _____. Most rivers enter the sea in tidal _____. Sand, shingle, mud or silt will be exposed along the estuary sides when the tide goes down.

(Adapted from *The Ordnance Survey Map Skills Book* by Chris Warn, 1986.)

These words may help you. You will not need all the words on this list.

estuaries, bends, meanders, flood, springs, tops, summits, gullies, ox-bow, eyots, sandbanks, rapids, torrents, tributaries, mouth.

Sequencing

Our experience suggests that this strategy is less frequently adopted. There are, however, several opportunities in the humanities to use it. Sequential thinking is clearly important, for example, in the study of history. Arranging things in the right order is an important aim for children who are studying this subject. Sequential thinking also has applications in religious education and geography. The technique is simple. The teachers write and make copies of several statements relating to a topic. The statements are then cut up. The children, individually, or preferably in groups, then sequence the statements into the correct order. This is particularly useful for children who have learning difficulties.

With a class of high achievers, for example, a teacher might use diagrams on the chalkboard to explain to the pupils how a barge goes uphill on a canal by using a lock. The children's task might then be to write in plain and unambiguous English a step-by-step guide to using a lock for pleasure canal users in this century. The teacher would explain the dire consequences for safety and loss of thousands of gallons of water if the instructions were written incorrectly. Experience suggests that the quality of work which high achievers produce on this task is extremely high. For a class of low achievers, however, such an approach is likely to lead to confusion. A different strategy might yield better results. In the first instance, if possible, the teacher would arrange to take the children to see a working lock, watch barges going through, and explain what was happening. Back in the classroom the teacher would then use the method outlined above to aid sequential thinking.

Example 6.2

The teacher would produce the following statements and cut them up. The pupils would be given an accompanying page of diagrams which would show the correct sequence. The pupil task would be to match the statements to the diagrams.

TITLE
How to go uphill on a canal

- When the water level in the lock is the same as the level of the upper level, Gate B is opened. Gate A stays shut. The barge sails out onto the upper level.
- The sluices by Gate B are opened. The lock slowly fills with water, raising the barge.

- The barge comes to the lock on the lower level.
- The barge sails into the lock and Gate A is shut behind it.

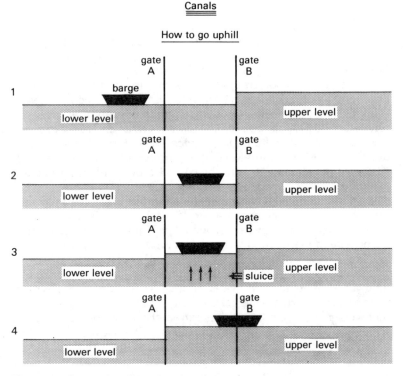

Figure 6.1 Sequencing diagram

Extension work might then be to ask pupils in groups to design some instructions for barges going from the upper level to the lower level with the children drawing their own diagrams. This lesson has been found to be extremely popular with children who have learning difficulties.

Equally this method of sequencing which gives children an important reason for reading can be used to put stages in the development of an historical event in the correct order. Well suited to this technique are the events of 1065–66 which led to the Battle of Hastings. The teacher may well have used the Bayeux Tapestry before this lesson to introduce the topic, and would probably have used maps to explain the main points of the story. The maps and other work would be available during the course of this assignment to which the class could refer.

Example 6.3

The pupil task, again working in groups, would be to put these events into the correct sequence:

- In 1065 Harold Godwinson was shipwrecked on the coast of Normandy.
- King Harold was beaten by William at the Battle of Hastings.
- Shortly after the Battle of Stamford Bridge King Harold had news that Duke William of Normandy had arrived with an army near Hastings.
- In 1066 Edward the Confessor died.
- King Harold marched north and defeated his brother and the King of Norway at the battle of Stamford Bridge.
- Probably Harold promised William of Normandy that he would help him to become the next King of England.
- When Edward died Harold Godwinson became King.
- King Harold marched south to meet Duke William near Hastings.
- On Christmas Day 1066, William of Normandy became King of England.
- Tostig and the King of Norway landed in Northern England. They wanted to take the English throne from Harold.

Realising that this is a complicated sequence of events this teacher had provided a number of clues in the statements, such as the dates, and connecting phrases such as 'shortly after the Battle of Stamford Bridge' to make the pupil task easier.

There is an almost infinite number of topics in humanities teaching which can be handled in this way, from the stages in urbanisation in geography, through to the events of the last week in Christ's life in religious education. Experience suggests that it is a neglected technique, but as a mean of prompting children with learning difficulties to read, and as a method of organising information it is probably unrivalled.

Prediction

This technique, in addition to aiding reading for learning, is very appropriate for use in humanities lessons. As its title suggests, it involves predicting possible outcomes from a passage which the children have already read. A passage is selected, or one is written by the teacher. The passage is then typed, if necessary, and duplicated so that the children have a copy each. If the reading level is considered too difficult for particular children with difficulties in reading, the passage can be put onto tape. The children are split into groups, they read the passage and where appropriate listen to the tape of it, while following the words at the same time. At the end they are asked to discuss 'What happens next'. This technique can be used at the beginning of a topic to bring out possible alternatives, or at the end when the children already know what did happen, to consider ways in which the course of action might have been different. Particularly, this technique is useful for the study of history as the following example demonstrates.

Example 6.4
The teacher prepared this information sheet on the events which followed the Wall Street Crash in the USA. The class, a bottom band, fourth year secondary, was split into groups, and was asked to predict what might happen next.

Roosevelt and the New Deal
In 1929 the Stock Exchange on Wall Street in the USA crashed. Many people lost their money. Some banks went bankrupt. Some people were thrown out of work.

The people who had no jobs had no money to spend on goods that were made. Less goods were needed so less goods were made. Companies made more people **redundant** because they did not need them to work anymore. Also these companies now needed less **raw materials** so many people who worked in the industries which got raw materials were made redundant. Less goods needed to be moved about the country so people who worked in transport were made redundant. People could not afford to pay rent or buy houses and had to live in **shanty towns** so less building workers were needed. By 1932, 13 million Americans were out of work.

The government of the time was run by Hoover. He was the President and he was a **Republican**. People thought he was not doing enough to help them. 'In Hoover we trusted, now we are busted' they said. They named the shanty towns after him. They became known as Hoovervilles.

In 1932, Roosevelt, a **Democratic** politican became President. He offered the American people a **New Deal**. He said he would get people back to work. To do this he decided to ...

Preparation for this part of the lesson was the watching of the BBC video 'Boom and Bust' which lasted twenty minutes and set the scene visually for this information sheet. The class had seen the 'Roaring Twenties' and had seen some of the reasons why the Wall Street Crash occurred. They had seen the effects of the crash and had heard at the end of the video 'Buddy, Can you spare a dime?' played over the scenes of depression and desperation.

This was a skilled piece of writing on the part of the teacher. New, important or difficult words were produced in bold type which highlighted them. In addition, the teacher had deliberately used 'redundant' and 'shanty town' again in the piece to reinforce their meaning. The readability level was such that the piece lay within the grasp of most of the class and the tape recording which had been made merely complemented their reading. For some, however, the tape recording was a vital addition to the information sheet.

The task of the pupils in groups of three was to try to predict what Roosevelt would have done to try to solve the problems caused by the depression. The discussion was slow to start, but the teacher moved round the groups making some suggestions to start it off. He asked the groups to concentrate on what had gone wrong to create the situation and what could be done to reverse the process. Eventually, some excellent learning, both in history and economics, occurred with many of the groups listing job creation initiatives which Roosevelt could have tried. The parallel with the 1980s was not lost on some of the class and discussion took place in one group of the difference between 'temporary' and created jobs, and 'real', permanent jobs.

The teacher's next lesson began with the video *The New Deal* and most children were interested to see how their own speculations matched up to what had happened during the 1930s.

Extracting and reorganising

This technique is important not only because it aids learning in the humanities but also because it is an essential skill for life beyond school. In reading a newspaper report an adult is extracting relevant and essential information and reorganising it so that it can assist their everyday existence. Adults do not bother, usually, to present the information they have extracted in another way. This intermediate stage is omitted. This technique gives children practice in the skill.

Essentially, children are given a written passage and asked to present the information they have extracted from it in another way, which might be in the form of a diagram, on a map, or in a mathematical chart. Experience suggests that this is a task which children enjoy doing and one which provides a fair degree of satisfaction. It also concentrates the pupils' minds on their reading.

There are many topics in the humanities that can effectively use this procedure. The migration of people into Britain at various stages in history is clearly a topic which can be dealt with by extracting information from the printed word and presenting it on a map. The decline in the manufacturing output of the Lancashire cotton industry is a geographical topic which can extract information from a book and present it on a bar chart. World population growth, equally, is a topic which can benefit from the same handling. For geography teachers interested in this type of work, a glance at a maths catalogue or a talk with colleagues in the maths department might provide many interesting applications as maths tries to spread across the curriculum as advocated in the Cockcroft Report (1982).

Other areas in the humanities can sensibly use an approach which extracts information from books or school prepared information sheets and asks the children to present it in a visual way, in the form of a diagram. Teachers often use this technique for designing pictorial revision aids or for producing teaching material to go on the wall. Instead of teachers doing this themselves they could productively ask the class to do it for them. An interesting project, for example, on life in Tudor England could involve groups of children within the class working on different aspects of Tudor life and producing visual materials to go on the wall or on an overhead projector. At some stage groups would be given an opportunity to talk to the class by using their prepared materials. In this way the printed word has been read, analysed by the children and presented both in a pictorial and verbal form.

At its most simple, however, this technique can be used for single lessons, as in this example.

Example 6.5

As part of a unit on 'work' this geography teacher was exploring industrial relations with a mixed-ability group of second years. In discussing the problems of workers' discontent, and ways in which these are avoided she was using a passage from a textbook about workers in the Fiat car factory in Turin. She asked the class to read the information and then draw a diagram to show the advantages of working for this company, according to the views of this worker. Because some of the children had learning difficulties the teacher drew an outline for the diagram to start them off.

> I like to work for the Fiat car company. They give me good pay of 300.000 lire a month. I also have a nice apartment in Turin built by the company. At the moment I am buying a transistor radio for my wife, a motor scooter for my son and a 'Mirafiori' for myself, all on a low cost hire-purchase plan that the company operates.
>
> I still play for the company football team but there are many other sports I could play at the Fiat Sports Club – and my teenage children get their amusements at the company youth recreation centre. I've got no complaints about Fiat – they taught me my job at the Fiat apprentice school and ever since have looked after my welfare in a

large number of ways – for instance, when I am sick I can go to the company medical centre.

My family has benefited – at the moment my son is at the Fiat holiday camp in the Alps. But you must excuse me – I'm just off to play my saxophone in the Fiat Jazz Band!

Arrivederci!

(From P. McCleod, *A Place to Work*)

The sort of diagrams which the children produced are shown in Figure 6.2.

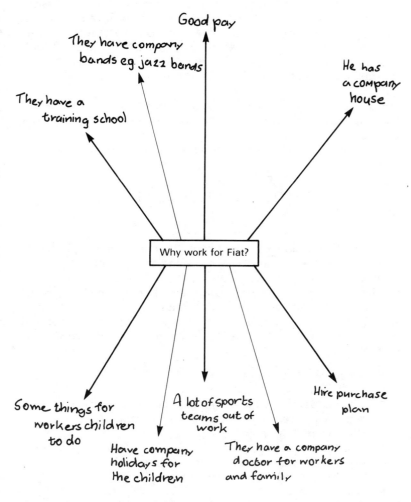

Figure 6.2 'Why I like working for Fiat'

This technique can also be used in history lessons. Instead of asking questions about working conditions in the early Industrial Revolution one teacher gave a series of headings which described various aspects of work. Children found this interesting since much of the preparation was a discussion of the sort of things people in our time were interested in when they went for a job.

Example 6.6
The children's task was to go through a simple information sheet about working conditions during the period of the Industrial Revolution and complete their own sheet according to how the various criteria were satisfied. The information sheet (not repro-duced here) contained some primary evidence in the form of prints of working life from the period under discussion and in the form of records of admissions to Manchester Infirmary because of indust-rial accidents.

Moreover, the introductory paragraph on the sheet was carefully read through with the children and care was taken that everyone understood what they had to do.

The work was done with a bottom band, third-year secondary school class.

WORKING CONDITIONS IN THE EARLY INDUSTRIAL REVOLUTION

People who worked in factories, mines and mills in the early Industrial Revolution were not very different from people today. They were interested in much the same things when it came to finding a job. They wanted a good wage. They also wanted good conditions. Here is a list of things you might be interested in if you went for a job when you left school. Read through the information sheet and fill in each section. You are building up a picture of how working life must have been for people in the Industrial Revolu-tion.

- What were their wages like?
- How did their employer treat them?
- What happened if they were ill or had an accident at work?
- What happened if they made a mistake at work?
- What were their holidays?
- Was there a pension scheme?
- What about tea breaks and breaks for meals?
- What hours did they have to work?
- Was the workplace safe?
- Were there any promotion prospects?

- Were they allowed to join a Trade Union?

Some of the children needed help with this exercise. For example, some had difficulty in reading 'promotion prospects' and had some trouble in understanding the concept. The teacher thought that it was sensible to include these words and the concept because, in Brennan's terms, that the children should read and comprehend them was a real and relevant objective for all the children in the class.

Readability

Clearly it is not sensible to give to children with learning difficulties texts, information sheets, or worksheets which they cannot use. Using the same textbook as a 'general reader' for all pupils within a mixed-ability class is likely, for example, to frustrate two groups within the class – the best readers and the poorest readers. This does not mean to say that textbooks cannot be used to good effect with whole classes; merely that they cannot be the basis of all work involving reading for that class. Children with learning difficulties at secondary schools can be many years behind their chronological reading ages and to be presented for lesson after lesson with an incomprehensible textbook is a clear cause both of failure and frustration.

It is sensible, therefore, to seek a method that teachers can use to assess the appropriateness of material. Tests exist which will tell teachers the readability of a text and these tests are useful tools for the teacher in selecting which books to buy or in deciding which pieces of their home produced stock they may sensibly give to particular groups of children.

However, the whole area of the readability of texts is confused. Tests are useful but their results should complement the professional judgements of the teachers and the judgement of the children. Children, in any case, will soon demonstrate if they have been given inappropriate material. While research suggests that teachers vary by up to seven years in their estimates of the age at which an average pupil can read a passage with understanding (Harrison, 1980), most teachers would be able to predict with a reasonable degree of accuracy whether particular children they teach would be able to cope with a particular passage. Nevertheless, it is useful for teachers to be aware of the wide range of tests available, be competent in administering them and to know what criteria make for easier or more difficult reading. All of these can help teachers to be more effective when they come to write their own material and less profligate in the buying of sets of books.

Limitations of readability tests with which teachers should be aware include the following.

1. Children can often show a remarkable facility to read something which really grasps their attention. Often the way in which a piece is written, the way it holds the attention and the excitement generated can increase the child's ability to read it. Moreover, the layout of a book can also encourage children to read, whereas a duller format might have the opposite effect.

2. As is set out below, readability tests usually concentrate on sentence length and syllable counts. Such tests are not competent to deal with the content of the piece. It may be, for example, that the word 'Manchester' appears several times in a piece which a geography teacher has written about transport networks in northern England. For a child who lives in Manchester this word will probably present little difficulty. The word still counts as three syllables in the test and increases the level of difficulty of the piece, when in reality the inclusion of the word Manchester in the test does not increase its difficulty for this particular child.

3. In addition, readability formulae do not give any indication as to the number of ideas which are encased in the text – a crucial factor as to the degree to which words which have been read can be understood. Kintsch (1974) suggested that a propositional analysis would be a better way of ensuring an accurate description of the difficulty of a piece of text. Also, as Arkell (1982) has pointed out with regard to the usefulness of readability tests in history texts, the tests cannot reveal the number or sophistication of the ideas in the text. The problem with this method is that, as Wilson (1985) suggested, it is very time consuming. However, teachers should take account of the 'density of ideas' as they review books or their own work.

4. There are a number of tests available. These include Fog, Flesch, Smog, Powers–Sumner–Kearl and Forcast. Clearly, they produce different results. The obvious difficulty is that the teacher has no ready-made guidelines to decide which test to use or which results to take. If the teacher only administers one test, it takes some time and many uses of the test for the teacher to be able to interpret the results in a practical way i.e. what do these results actually mean in terms of learning outcomes for a particular class or child?

Our advice to teachers is to dispense with any one particular test and to use, instead, a computer program which will amalgamate the result of a number of readability formulae and produce a combined figure made up of those results which the program considers to be most significant. 'Readlevel', for example is one such program. It simply involves typing in a number of words, taken from the beginning, the middle and the end of a piece, and the text will be graded for its readability. It will ask the user to continue typing in words until it has enough to give an accurate figure although a read out can be obtained at any time.

Another advantage of this program is that it is far less time-consuming than tests which are manually administered. Those wishing to continue with an old technology of calculators and long division can see how to operate a Flesch test with geography textbooks in Boardman (1982). They can see there the sort of calculations involved. Those preferring a more modern approach should pester their special needs department to buy a cheap software program that can be used by the whole school to perform this important task.

Example 6.7
'Readlevel' in operation on a teacher's home produced notes.
The following is from a teacher's printed notes and is an introduction to a GCSE case study on the Battle of Britain. The original was written on a word processor. It was written by the teacher in a 'natural' style intended for pupils who would do well in GCSE history and who had no problems with reading. The teacher, then, in an effort to achieve differentiation in this work, attempted to be sensitive to the needs of poor readers, and intended to produce a similar booklet on the Battle of Britain with the same maps, the same cartoons, and photographs but with a text with a considerably lower reading age.

The task was fairly time consuming, but, stored on disk, was work which could be used in future years, and, if necessary, improved in the light of consumer criticism.

The technique was simple. Using the software program 'Readlevel' the original text was analysed and found to have a reading-ease level of 53 – fairly difficult – much too difficult for children who struggle with reading. The next stage involved going through the original text, sentence by sentence on computer monitor and changing it to reduce its level of difficulty. This was achieved by reducing the length of the sentences and the incidence of three syllable or more words. Most tests of readability concentrate on these two criteria.

The final stage was to check a sample of the new text on the 'Readlevel' program. The new text had a reading ease level of 81 – easy. Notionally, the basic ideas had been accessed to children who previously would have found this material far too difficult and probably would have become frustrated by their inability to handle it.

Below is the original test with the 'relatively difficult' reading level. The revised text follows on p. 127.

BACKGROUND

After the declaration of war on Germany by Britain and France on 3 September 1939, Britain and France themselves were unable to do anything to prevent the fall of Poland in October 1939. From then, until the following spring, the war was quiet. Massive industrial conversion from peacetime to wartime continued, the RAF dropped leaflets on Berlin attempting to persuade the Germans to end the war, and cardboard coffins were stockpiled in East London to cope with the expected casualties from the bombing which the British were convinced would occur. Meanwhile, the French sat secure (in their view) behind their **Maginot Line**. The Germans planned their future campaigns. There was, however, little happening which could be thought of as war. No battles were being fought, no cities bombed and there was no sign of the early activity which had marked the start of the First War in 1914. This period of inactivity is frequently known as the **'Phoney War'**.

The war began in earnest in the spring of 1940. On **8 April 1940**, Hitler launched his attack on Denmark and Norway and they were overrun easily. The German army, or **Wehrmacht**, was using techniques planned in the 1930s and rehearsed against Poland called **Blitzkrieg** or 'lightning war' – a war based on speed and surprise using motorised units of tanks and infantry following. The British attempted to save the iron ore supplies from Sweden which came to the coast at Narvik and for a time British forces held Narvik. Eventually they were forced to withdraw, although Britain had managed to destroy some German ships.

In the row which took place over Hitler's conquest of Norway in the House of Commons, the Prime Minister, Neville Chamberlain, was forced to resign and was replaced by Winston Churchill on **10 May 1940**. On the same day, the Germans launched their long expected attack in the West – on Holland, Belgium, and France. Using paratroops, dive bombers, and tanks the battles were short lived and quickly the Germans burst through the enemy defences. The theory of tank warfare had been developed by Guderian in the 1930s and now it was put into good practice. The tanks pushed through to the Channel ports and the infantry followed to mop up behind. The French were quickly defeated. The British Expeditionary Force in France, led by Lord Gort, seeing that the French were beyond help, deserted them and made for the port of Dunkirk. Here it was surrounded by the Germans but in the 'miracle of Dunkirk' a whole armada of small ships came from Britain and in six days rescued 300,000 servicemen.

Readlevel results
* FOG: 18 years 6 months
  SMOG: 17 years 0 months
  POWERS–SUMNER–KEARL: 11 years 7 months
  FORCAST: 15 years 8 months
* FLESCH: 17 years 0 months
* READING EASE SCORE: 53 – Fairly difficult

Multisyllabic words: 37
Words per sentence: 21
Syllables per 100 words: 155

---

*Relevant ratings for this text

Revised text:
BACKGROUND
On 3 September 1939, Britain and France declared war on Germany. They could not stop the Germans in Poland. In October Poland fell. Not much happened until spring 1940. Both sides built more weapons. They stopped making other things. The RAF dropped leaflets on Berlin. They said Germany should end the war. Cardboard coffins were placed in East London. It was thought that many people would die if the German dropped bombs. Most people thought this would happen.

At the same time the French did nothing. They felt safe in the **Maginot Line**. The Germans planned what to do next. It was not like the First World War. That had begun with battles. Now, nothing happened. This time in 1939–1940 is known as the **Phoney War**.

The battles began in spring 1940. On **8 April**, Hitler attacked Denmark and Norway. They were easily beaten. The German army, or **Wehrmacht**, used a new way of fighting. It was used against Poland. It was called **Blitzkrieg** or 'lightning war'. It used speed and surprise. Tanks cut the defences. Infantry followed. The British tried to save the iron ore supplies from Sweden. These came to the coast at Narvik. For a time British forces held Narvik. Later they were forced to pull out. Britain had been able to destroy some German ships.

There was a row in the House of Commons. Many MPs thought the troops should have done better in Norway. The Prime Minister, Neville Chamberlain, was forced to resign. He was replaced by Winston Churchill on **10 May 1940**. On the same day, the Germans launched their long expected attack in the West. This was against

Holland, Belgium, and France. They used paratroops, dive bombers, and tanks. The battles were short. Quickly the Germans burst through the enemy defences. The ideas the Germans used to fight using tanks had been thought out by **Guderian**. The idea worked. The tanks pushed through to the Channel ports. Then the infantry followed to mop up behind. The French were quickly defeated. The **British Expeditionary Force** in France, led by Lord Gort, saw that the French were beyond help. They left them and made for the port of Dunkirk. Here they were surrounded by the Germans. In the 'miracle of Dunkirk' a large number of small ships came from Britain. In six days they rescued 300,000 servicemen.

Readlevel results
* FOG: 10 years 1 month
* SMOG: 11 years 0 months
* POWERS–SUMNER–KEARL: 9 years 8 months
  FORCAST: 14 years 11 months
* FLESCH: 11 years 11 months
* READING EASE SCORE: 81 – Easy

Multisyllabic words: 19
Words per sentence: 6
Syllables per 100 words: 140

---

*Relevant ratings for this text

This example provides several illustrations of the points made above. In the first place the tests vary markedly in their scores for the two texts. In the second place, the program disregards some of the test for its read-out of a reading ease level. Moreover, if the same information is enclosed in the new text, as this teacher has tried to do, it is often impossible to reduce the level of difficulty to that appropriate for the poorest readers. By continuing to include the words which this teacher regarded as important for the study of this historical period, e.g. Guderian, paratroops, servicemen, etc., the reading ease level, though improved, would still have troubled a very poor reader. In this instance, the teacher would have to take other steps such as putting the piece on tape. What is more, the limitations of exercises of this type are easily seen. By reducing the number of multisyllabic words and shortening the sentences, the style of writing has suffered. It has become jerky and no longer flows. Unless the writing is very skilled and unless a long time is spent in its composition this is an almost inevitable consequence of the exercise.

Our feeling is that the process is still valuable provided that the reading material is not the only resource in the classroom for the treatment of the topic under discussion. If the teacher had shown a video, done some map work, organised the class in looking at photographs, and then produced this information sheet for the pupils to work with, then the style of the piece would be less relevant. To use this resource solely, however, would make for a very arid and tedious lesson.

Sophisticated testing of this sort is not the only type of testing that can be done to judge the appropriateness of printed texts for particular pupils. Another informal method is available which has the advantage of encouraging pupil/teacher interaction. It is based on the ideas set out in Chapter 4 on Independent, Instructional and Frustrational levels. On the basis that there is no point in giving children material to read which is either too easy or too difficult it is possible to ask children to read something from a book. The ease with which they can complete this task will tell the teacher whether the book is appropriate or not. Experience suggests that children will readily take part in this, provided that the reason for it is shared with them. It gives to them the idea that the teacher cares sufficiently in their learning to take the trouble to discover what is appropriate material.

Views differ as to what constitutes each of the levels but we concur with Cavan's view, i.e. that if children make no more than 1 error in every 100 words in the reading, and can comprehend 90 per cent of the material then they are at an independent level. This may mean that material which stretches them a little more should be introduced. If children make 5 mistakes in every 100 words and are found after teacher questioning to comprehend 75 per cent of the passage then they are at the instructional level and will need support and guidance with the material. Nevertheless this is the material that they should be using. If, on the other hand, children make more than 10 errors in every 100 words and they understand less than half of the content of the piece the material is too difficult and should be put back in the stock room. These children are at the frustrational level and easier material should be found or produced for them.

This method is time consuming but will work, providing that teachers keep adequate records on what sort of material children with learning difficulties have been using successfully in the past. If they have this information it should be possible to predict fairly accurately which material will be useful and which will not. However, it is not feasible to use this method with standard textbooks that come from publishers. For these the Readlevel approach is much more appropriate and teachers are advised to use it. Occasionally, books which are advertised as being 'for low attainers' have little practical application in the classroom for this population.

COMPUTERS

Teachers and word processors

Irrespective of the issue of readability the previous example does show the benefits of the word processor as an aid for teachers in their preparation. The teacher had the original text in front of him on the screen and simply changed it sentence by sentence by using the 'delete' keys. At the end of the task it was simply a matter of printing out and saving the revised version. Notionally, it would be possible to produce a range of differentiated material in this way and to ask children to self-select colour coded levels of difficulty. All work could be stored on disk in the school's reprographic room or resource centre and retrieved and duplicated by a clerical assistant when required without the teacher having to do anything except to give enough notice for the work to be carried out. This is the way forward for humanities departments that seek a greater level of sophistication and wish to maximise the opportunities for time saving and better quality material that modern technology allows.

The development of the use of micro-processors in secondary schools has been one of the most significant in the last 15 years. Schools, LEAs, the DES, and the DTI have invested heavily in hardware. In some schools the opportunities presented by this technological revolution have not been grasped as firmly as they might. While many teachers of humanities subjects are aware of a variety of software packages for their classes, our experience suggests that humanities teachers have not, in the main, developed the computer's use for themselves and their departments. This is a crucial area generally in humanities departments and is especially important in the preparation of work for children with learning difficulties.

Sensible use of a micro-processor has many benefits for teachers involved in record keeping and preparing work for children of all abilities. This is increasingly likely to be the case as more humanities departments move to new methods of assessment involving the use of profiles which can be easily stored and coded on a disk. However, it is in the preparation of work that the micro comes into its own with children who have learning difficulties.

In the first instance it is axiomatic that children with learning difficulties need materials that are well presented. Materials need to be well set out; written material ideally should be typed or produced on a word processor. It is our view that each humanities department in secondary schools should possess its own cheap micro, capable of word processing materials for use by children. If material is poorly presented it is no wonder that work which children themselves do should demonstrate the same quality.

The word processor is a flexible tool, allowing changes to be made to material which did not work. It allows the teacher to insert fresh material into an older piece of work, and the potential for the storage of material is obvious. However, in attempting to produce differentiated work for classes, especially mixed-ability groups, it really comes into its own. Essentially, it is much easier to ensure that the same sense remains after the words have been changed to make them more appropriate for children who read at different levels.

Micro-processors

Apart from the important uses which word processors have for teachers, micro-processors also have tremendous applicability for children, especially those with learning difficulties. As a motivating factor the computer may well be the most important aid in the classroom. There is much evidence to support this.

> The teleprinter exercised a hypnotic effect which I have never since been able to emulate in the classroom.
>
> (Kinloch, 1985, p. 172)

and,

> although there might be criticism of the expensive use of gimmickry, I believe that we ought to use whatever resources are available to motivate such pupils providing we are working towards a deeper historical understanding. Pupils who normally show little interest in the most well conceived multi-media presentation, can be triggered by the computer.
>
> (Smith, 1985, p. 112)

Equally, Rea wrote of the power of reinforcement of learning which the micro can provide:

> Of course it took them longer to type in their records, but once they realized the magic of the delete key and when they were shown that we could correct mistakes or add or remove a record using the edit command, even after the file was finished, they relaxed and made very few errors. The joy on the face of William, (whose writing on paper was very immature, however hard he tried) when he noticed

that on the screen his records looked exactly the same as those of the most able child, made it all worthwhile. I found that the computer also improved the concentration and retention span of the children.

(Rea, 1985, p. 26)

As with all resources, the computer must be the servant of the teacher. There is a temptation, especially with computers, which are relatively new technology in schools, to regard them with some apprehension and possibly with too much respect. They are powerful aids but the same rules must apply to their use as to that of any other resource and the teacher intending to use one should ask him or herself the same questions.

- Is what I'm trying to do, by using this resource, appropriate to the children?
- Does the computer aid the attainment of teaching objectives?
- Applying the principle of 'minimum intervention' is there another, less time consuming way, involving less disruption of the timetable, in which I could have achieved precisely the same result?

There are several uses to which the computer may be put to facilitate greater learning and there are several objectives, especially in humanities, which cannot be reached by children, as easily, without using the computer. In the first instance, the computer is a marvellous tool for presenting children's work in a 'professional' way. While humanities teachers, like all teachers, would not abandon their responsibilities for such cross curricular goals as the improvement of handwriting, this is not the primary function of humanities teaching. A central theme throughout this book is that humanities subjects have much more to offer the child with learning difficulties than practice in the 'basic skills'. The computer offers an opportunity for children to produce work of a high standard, simply because what they write can be printed out.

There are three main ways in which this can be done.

1.   Teachers should encourage children to use the word processing function of the micro. This is connected to our thoughts above about micros and teacher use. Children will see much more point in learning a word processing package if, round the school, they see teachers using word processors and see much of the printed material which arrives on their desks having been word processed by their teachers. The word processor gives the child for whom spelling and writing do not come easily a chance to produce a perfect copy. The

technique is simple. The child produces a first draft and prints it out. The teacher makes corrections to spelling, etc. and returns it to the child. The child reloads the file and, using the delete and insert keys, makes the necessary changes. The final, and hopefully perfect piece, is then printed. This removes from the task of producing a perfect piece of work the heartache and the frustrations caused by working slowly, by making other errors as the original ones are corrected as the child rewrites the piece by hand. The process is much quicker, the final product much more presentable.

2. Teachers should investigate the possibilities afforded by software packages which print children's work in a particular format. One of these, which experience suggests is a powerful motivator for children with learning difficulties is 'Frontpage'. As its name suggests, this simple program gives children an opportunity to write the front page of a newspaper. They give the paper a title, a price, and a date. They write a story and produce a picture, and write an advert. This is an extremely useful package for the teaching of 'events'. It can be used to explore controversial local issues with rival groups attempting to convince their 'readers' of a particular point of view on the building of a by-pass, or a supermarket. It can be used in religious studies to catalogue an important event in one of the world's great religions. Equally, in history, it offers an attractive opportunity for children to chronicle an important event which they have been studying through a variety of other sources. Of course, children have to be taught to 'suspend their disbelief' that many of the events could have been reported in a newspaper in the historical time they have been studying, but the eagerness with which children with learning difficulties produce their work suggests that it is a productive way to display the results of their researches.

3. Teachers may explore the possibilities offered by the concept keyboard. This peripheral, which is an alternative to the traditional keyboard, has many educational uses. Essentially, words, pictures or diagrams are placed by the teacher on the 'keyboard' which is an A4 or A3 sized pad. When the child presses a particular picture or word a related word or picture will appear on the screen. This technology is especially useful for children whose difficulties are more severe or those with physical impairments but it also has a more general applicability. Some interesting work in this area has been developed by the Learning Support Department of Burnage High School, Manchester. A brief description of the work done

here may give teachers thoughts about how their own humanities resources could be extended using the concept keyboard.

Several overlays pertinent to humanities learning were produced. One represented aspects of the Celtic Hill Fort which was built on the present site of Manchester Cathedral. The overlay consisted mainly of pictures. As children pressed each of the pictures of the fort, simple notes about it appeared on the screen. As they progressed round the keyboard, a series of important statements were built up and, at the end, a print-out could be obtained. Apart from the obvious benefits in presenting information about the fort in an interesting way, the program also assisted children in developing the skills of notemaking and summarising information.

Two pieces encouraging the development of skills in geography were also produced on the concept keyboard, both involving maps. The first was a map of the North West taken from an old road atlas. A series of descriptions of various places on the map was printed at its side. The children's task was to match the descriptions to the places, and press the town on the keyboard. When the town, for example, Fleetwood, was pressed and matched with 'Fishing Port', a message appeared on the screen to inform children of their success. In another instance, an Ordnance Survey map was placed over the concept keyboard. The children's task in the same way was to match a series of descriptions with the appropriate OS symbols by touch. Again success was flashed on the screen. Simple information about how to construct similar programs for the concept keyboard using the 'Touch Explorer' program can be found in Dyke (1986). These initiatives were reported in the Newsletter of the Manchester Special Education Microelectronics Resource Centre (SEMERC) (Martin, 1987). There are three other SEMERCs – in Newcastle, Bristol, and Redbridge. Humanities teachers may find other information which is of use to them in these centres.

Issues of classroom organisation

Schools have made a variety of responses to the organisational issues involved in the introduction of computers. How the school has organised this resource had crucial importance for the use to which they can be put. In some schools each department may have a machine. In this case, if a micro is available for most of the day it should be used for most of the day. It is appropriate in such a situation for the micro to be used by individual children or a small group of children while the rest of the class does something else. In the case, above, for example, children might well work with their resources to produce the newspaper story of the despatch of the fireships into the Spanish fleet at Calais in 1588, and then wait their turn to use the 'Frontpage' program to produce their article. Inherent in this are problems of classroom organisation, or too many groups wanting to use the single machine at the same time, or children rushing to be the first on the computer. Teachers need to be sensitive to these difficulties and develop strategies for follow-up work to keep children occupied while others are using the machine.

Other schools have placed all their machines in one room and staff have to compete for time in the room. There are occasions when humanities teachers need a room of this type when children, in groups, are working three to a machine. Clearly the use of a room of this sort is a question which needs to be discussed across the school. Perhaps a booking system, similar to that used for the video camera may be in operation. Competing claims of departments who need the room as part of GCSE examination work will have to be considered. It is, however, the function of the heads of departments of faculties in humanities to make out a sufficiently strong case for time on the machines that these claims are considered and acknowledged by senior management. Clearly the room will not be available at all times when humanities teachers would wish to use it. The use of the computer therefore needs to be well planned to dovetail neatly into the work that is being pursued in the general classroom. Computer lessons need to be seen by children as an integral part of a process which leads towards positive learning outcomes, not merely as a 'treat' which occurs periodically.

Ideally, perhaps, each department needs a single micro that can be used by children during the course of the school day and access to a room in which there are ten or more machines. Neither of these is adequate on its own to meet the needs of humanities teachers.

Commercial programs for humanities teaching

There are a great number and variety of programs for use in humanities classrooms. It is not our rôle to list them or to point, in detail, to those which may have particular applicability for children with learning difficulties. Instead we intend to describe the sorts of things which programs do and to suggest how they may be used. Teachers' best strategy, subsequently, is to explore LEA provision for reviewing software. Some, for example, have computer centres where teachers can work through programs, using their professional judgements and the knowledge of their own children to decide on appropriateness. LEAs also will have bought a licence to copy some software programs and should have a list of these. Essentially, then, in many cases, programs can be made available to schools without charge, except for the cost of the disk onto which they are copied and the charge for photocopying the documentation.

Questions which should be uppermost in the minds of teachers when considering using a program with children who have learning difficulties are:

1. Have the children sufficient experience of computers to cope with basic tasks such as switching the machine on, loading disks, feeding paper, etc.? Are they sufficiently aware of where individual keys are on the keyboard, especially the RETURN and SPACE BAR keys? Many machines, for example, do not name the SPACE on the keyboard yet many programs require its use. Do they know what may happen if the CAPS LOCK or SHIFT LOCK are on? Do they know what the cursor is or what the ARROW KEYS are? All these are important for using the machine and failure to understand them can lead to a speedy loss of motivation. If teachers doubt that children are going to be defeated by the basic operation of the machine, perhaps a list of simple instructions tied by string to the computer table is the answer.

2. Do the children have all the necessary pre-skills to cope with the program? For example, are the instructions which appear on the screen, clear and of a reading level which is appropriate to the children? This is a major problem for children with learning difficulties with much commercially produced software. Comments made earlier in this chapter should assist teachers interested in appropriate reading levels. (As with some adults, children can easily be frightened off computers if their first few experiences leave them baffled!)

3. If there is any supporting material to which the children will be directed during the program, is it pitched at an appropriate level or will it have to be modified before the children begin?

4. Is the particular program entirely connected with the scheme of work the children are following or will it leave them confused because it is really about something different? Teachers should consider how well the program fits in with the work already done and the work which is to be done. Many programs will suggest follow up work.

5. For what objectives is the program appropriate? Many programs are multi-faceted. They are capable of being used at different levels and even a program which can be useful for

high achievers at GCSE may, nevertheless, have some applicability for younger children who have difficulties.

6. Is the program sufficiently exciting for the children? The answer to this will vary. Children in some schools will be used to working with computers and will be used to seeing exciting graphics. Some may have systems at home. If the program which they are asked to use in school lacks vitality their motivation may suffer considerably.

7. Are there any supplementary resources which teachers should prepare before the lesson in the computer room? If time in the room is limited the teacher has to have it right on the first occasion. There is less opportunity than in the general classroom to see that some children are finding something difficult because the teacher had not anticipated that an extra aid would be needed. In the general classroom the teacher can always prepare it for the following lesson. In the computer room the next lesson might be some weeks away by which time the opportunity may have been lost.

8. If the class is of mixed ability, how are the children going to be grouped for computer work? Experience suggests that it is better to ensure that the children with learning difficulties are spread around the groups. Even children who cannot read functionally have made excellent contributions to group work round the computer when their imagination has been fired. One of the other children reads from the screen, another makes any recording on paper which is necessary while all the members of the group discuss the next stage. It is usually unnecessary for the teacher to organise this. The children will do it themselves. Working in groups, interactively with a computer is one of the most productive learning situations that teachers can organise for children whose reading is poor.

Example 6.8

Viking England – The Raiders: Fernleaf Educational Software

This program is one of four, all part of the same package which consider various aspects of Viking England. The program which we have chosen to address is the one which deals with a voyage across the North Sea from Scandinavia to Britain.

The program is menu driven. This is computer jargon, simply meaning that when teachers have loaded the program from the disk into the machine the program runs itself; it does not need the disk to remain in the drive. The teacher therefore only needs one disk. This can be used to load the program into all the machines before the class arrives.

Essentially the program sets up a decision-making exercise. The pupils have to sail across the sea, taking with them stores, men, and horses; land at a sensible place; build camps; send out scouts; discover sites worthy of attack; attack them and return home within 90 days. A slightly false atmosphere is created by use of a godlike figure called the 'Thing'. This sets the parameters of the exercise. Children may not make certain decisions because the 'Thing' will not allow it. This device prevents the game being truly historical in nature and also has confused some children with learning difficulties, who do not understand what it is about particular decisions which prohibit them in this way and what the consequences are for their own decisions of the intervention and unpredictability of the 'Thing'.

The reading level of the instructions which appear on the screen is easy enough for most pupils to comprehend what it is they have to do next. The information sheet needs some modifications and some explanations before everyone can understand it. Some words, such as Runic Stones, will require explanation. Moreover, the descriptions used by the information sheet to describe the various places where the Vikings can land need to be re-written for poor readers.

It is helpful if the teacher has prepared the class in advance with some basic information. It is also helpful if the children are familiar with the map of Britain and the west coast of northern Europe. They, also would benefit from an information sheet on the weather of the North Sea.

An element of excitement is introduced during the voyage when weather can intervene and sink some of the ships. Also, if the children have not packed enough food, men will die of starvation if the voyage is too long. The teacher walking round the groups will need to talk to children about why this has happened.

Children with learning difficulties need a supplementary sheet to explain what various map symbols mean to assist them in choosing a good landing place and discussion before they begin the program is needed to explain on which sorts of shore it is difficult to land a boat.

Some preparatory work is also needed on why the Vikings travelled to Britain, what sort of plunder they captured and from which people they captured it. Additionally children, at one stage, have to decide how many men to send on a raid and how many will stay to guard camp. Often large numbers are involved. In some other programs, e.g. 'Fletcher's Castle' again written by Fearnleaf, the subtraction is done by the machine. In this program, however, the children have to do it. Certain children with learning difficulties will not cope very well with taking 83 from 151, and the provision of calculators would help. Only by reviewing the software very carefully can teachers decide what aids will be needed.

Many of the programs designed for use with history classes are simulations of this type — essentially games with decision-making exercises built into them. Some, like 'Into the Unknown' from Tressell Publications, though similar, are the focus of a whole teaching unit involving historical, geographical, economic and religious studies. In addition, databases containing census returns and local records are of great use in the history classroom.

In geography, map work is an area which can be addressed very well by using computers. 'Mapstart', produced by Longmans, is ideal for teaching essential skills of map reading, including work on symbols, direction and scale. There are also a number of simulation games, involving transport systems and the problems of various industries.

Example 6.9

The Fishing Game: Netherhall Software

The game is played by a group of up to four children, each taking the part of a trawler captain out of a different port. The winner is the captain who makes the most profit from a season's fishing in the waters round Britain. The program has been very well researched, with great efforts made to ensure the accuracy of figures. The documentation is excellent, and the handbook goes some way towards providing information for its use for children with learning difficulties. Since the program is not menu driven, it requires a partial copy to be made on disk for each machine being used.

The program deals with direction and bearing and is sophisticated enough to provide for differentiation in the mixed-ability class. Children may enter compass points, e.g. south-south-west or north-east, to tell the computer where they want the trawler to go. In addition, the program can work in degrees. The teacher, then, has the flexibility to organise the lesson in the computer room in different ways. The highest achievers can play the game using nothing but bearings in degrees. Less good geographers can use bearings in terms of compass points. For children with difficulties, the teacher can make a transparent overlay out of OHP transparencies on which the points of the compass are marked. The children can then place the transparency over the screen and find the correct bearing.

High achievers will have no difficulty in estimating distance on the map using the scale. Low achievers may have considerable difficulty. A teacher who was sensitive to this might well decide to make, in advance of this lesson, lengths of wood that corresponded, on the scale which the program uses, to 50 miles, 100 miles, 200 miles, and 400 miles to give the children a concrete aid to work out distances involved (over-estimating distance results in running aground and a bill for salvage).

It is possible, then, by reviewing software carefully, to see what each program has to offer. Some programs are fairly rigid; others have the necessary flexibility to allow the teacher to select a range of teaching objectives and to work towards them. Some will be sufficiently simple to allow the program to be used as it stands; others will require the construction of concrete aids or other supplementary material if the teaching objectives are to be reached. Which ever is the case, the use of software programs by humanities teachers is too good an opportunity to be missed. As a method of achieving positive pupil outcomes, in some areas it is unrivalled.

VIDEOS AND TAPE RECORDERS

Watching videos

For the humanities teacher video and film is an indispensable part of teaching material. Film is the major method by which humanities teachers may import the world into their classrooms. A whole range of videos and films exists, and their number can be supplemented, almost weekly, by excellent television programmes. It seems impossible, for example, to imagine geography being taught without some use of video. If one simple aim of geography teaching is to introduce children to people from other places, there can be no better method. There is some debate as to the effectiveness of video, however. Many children are over-exposed to television and some teachers believe that the passive nature of television watching means that watching a video in a humanities lesson produces little learning.

Our experience suggests that videos used appropriately are an important additional resource to develop understanding and knowledge. In fact, all humanities departments in secondary schools should make the purchase of a 'play only' video for the use of their department a high priority. These machines are cheap when compared with the cost of a full set of textbooks and in our view have much greater applicability. Moreover, it is not sufficient to have access to the school's videos when a booking system may mean that the aid is not available for the precise lesson when it would have the greatest applicability. A booking system is necessary within the humanities department, of course, but negotiation and careful planning can eliminate most clashes.

There is little excuse for using video inappropriately. As Weber (1978) has pointed out: 'using film as a desperate safety valve or as a substitute for teaching is not good pedagogy' (p. 159). Videos that humanities teachers offer to children should be significant, an integral part of the course. They should not be used as fillers.

The advantages of using videos with classes that have within them children with learning difficulties is that it does not limit the audience. The whole class can experience the same stimulus. The class discussion can be based on a shared experience. The medium is immediate and familiar. In Chapter 1 we discussed the lack of knowledge by which the child with learning difficulties is frequently disadvantaged. The use of video can, if sensitively planned and handled, compensate to a degree. Watching a video about Hadrian's Wall does not depend on the family having a car, or on Uncle Arthur having a special interest in the Roman period. It does not even depend on the ability to read or write. It provides a shared experience for the class that can be discussed and explored. The 'picture' is not determined by the teacher's skills of description nor the pupils' past experience and ability to build an imaginary picture.

When using a video with pupils with learning difficulties there are a number of factors to consider:

- Teachers must have seen the film before they show it to the children. If this essential step has not been taken then the concepts or information that the teacher wishes to draw out cannot have been planned. This means, in addition, that follow-up work cannot be planned.
- Consistent with our general approach, children need to know *why* they are watching the video. This needs to be clearly stated. They need to be told what it is that the teacher wants them to learn. Offering pupils a 40 minute video and expecting children with special needs to be able to answer a set of questions about the whole video is likely to bore them. It should not be a memory test. If teachers are using video with older children it is best, if time permits, to show the video through once and then again. The second time the teacher can stop the video where questions need to be discussed.
- Some recorded programmes that are not produced specifically for schools' use, and even some that are, will contain too much information for pupils with learning difficulties to assimilate; the language may also be too complex and the vocabulary beyond their experience. This does not negate the use of the video especially if the class is mixed ability and

contains some children who will understand. Strategies can be built into the use of video so that understanding is ensured. These are three possible courses of action:

- The pause button must be used extensively. The video should be stopped and difficult or particularly important points should be elucidated by teacher talk or by discussion.
- With some videos the pictures have tremendous use for schools while the soundtrack is completely inappropriate. The obvious answer would be to dub a new, and easier soundtrack on to the original tape. This, however, infringes copyright and should not be attempted. It is, though, possible to turn down the sound entirely and play a tape recording of a teacher-designed soundtrack to accompany the 'silent' movie. This is extremely time consuming but if it is worth doing with particular films then it can be very successful in making the meaning behind the pictures intelligible to children with learning difficulties. Failing that, it is possible to talk over the pictures, although this creates a situation that is even more false.
- It is also possible, to set up situations where children with special needs can review a video by making use of a support teacher or welfare assistant while more able pupils are occupied with the follow-on work commensurate with their level of achievement.

- There is no need to show all of a particular film at once. One problem with videos is that they tend to dictate the pace and timing of the lesson. It is much better to select parts out of a particular film and show only them. If there is no time after the film has finished for discussion, either among the class or in groups, or for other follow-up work, much of the point of watching the film will have disappeared. Children should be encouraged to become good watchers of television and video. Observation is an essential skill in humanities and if teachers use the freeze-frame function and begin a discussion about one part of the video, much good work can be done.

Making videos (pupils)

Making videos offers a superb opportunity for pupils with learning difficulties. Many secondary schools now have access to a portable, or semi-portable video camera. This has a real educational function and should not be used solely for recording the school play to show at Parents' Evening. Of all the 'concrete' resources in schools it is the one which teachers of children with special needs should make their own. As part of a whole-school policy on the use of resources some schools allow teachers who intend to use the camera with children who have special needs a higher priority than teachers who do not. This is commendable practice. Among those benefits which children with learning difficulties receive from using a video camera in humanities lessons are these:

- There is a tremendous opportunity for co-operative learning. Children are faced with the task of apportioning work which is needed if the enterprise is to work.
- The video provides an excellent motivating factor. Much more effort and concentration usually go into written work which is going to form the script of a film than into other types of written work.
- The planning of the film offers the opportunity for the development of higher reading skills, such as sequencing. It also offers plenty of scope for the pupils to use research techniques.
- In the mixed-ability class, it provides an excellent opportunity for children with difficulties to be fully integrated as the sharing of tasks is perceived by the children to be essential to the completion of the task.
- Self esteem can be raised much more easily by using recording equipment especially when the film is shown to others.

However, there are some practical limitations.

- Children must know how to operate the machine if they are going to make their own film. This requires considerable training and much use to gain familiarity with the machine. In practice, it usually means that the teacher will have to set up the machine so that the pupils only have to aim and press the on/off switch. There is no need, unless children are especially interested, for the teacher to explain the complexities of the white/colour balance, etc.
- Video making is an activity which must involve small groups only. There is too much scope for children becoming bored if the group is over large thus making control difficult and ruining the experience for everyone.
- As with all other activities, the making of a film, however short, must have tight objectives. The work which the children do may well be fairly fluid but they must be aware of what the objectives are before they begin.

Making videos (teachers)

There are two important uses of the video camera and playback machine which teachers may adopt to facilitate positive outcomes in the learning of children with difficulties. Firstly, it is not always possible to find a commercially produced video which will deal, precisely, with something that is an integral part of a course. If at all practical, it is possible for the teacher to make a short video illustrating essential points. For example, if the timetable or transport problems made it impossible to take a group of children down to the local canal, it should be possible for the teacher to video a barge going through a lock and show this to the class.

It should be clear that, ideally, the child with learning difficulties needs to have ideas presented in as concrete a form as possible. If children are studying valleys then they should see a valley. If they are studying central business districts they should go and look at them. If they are trying to discover the essential characteristics of Judaism they might visit a synagogue. If they are talking about Roman villas in the classroom they should be taken to one. Humanities, as we have seen, has to import much of the world into the classroom artificially. It is better to take children out into it, or, when they are older, allow them to go on their own.

If this proves to be impossible then using a video of a site, though second best, is the nearest the teacher has to taking the children to see that site. The use of video for this sort of task is acceptable and the occasions on which it can be used to produce good resources in humanities, are almost endless. Clearly, as with the production of many resources, the task is time consuming, but it should be time well spent. It is not the same as going out of the classroom but it is better than relying on photographs. For example, to return to the question of how barges manage to go uphill: it is scarcely possible to explain this using photographs but a couple of hours spent making a video makes a complicated procedure intelligible to the child who has learning difficulties.

The other use to which video can be put is in the recording of children's work on rôle-play exercises. As will become clear in the section on micros, group work is an important teaching strategy to operate with children who have learning difficulties. Younger children especially are keen to see themselves on video and much of their best work in drama is done when the camera is present. Whether the work which they are doing concerns a mock board meeting of a company as part of a mini-enterprise project, a rôle-play exercise in which children take rôles as members of a Board of Health during a cholera epidemic, or some first year work where pupils design their own parts to demonstrate the working of the Saxon legal system, the experience will be enhanced by the use of the video camera.

As HMI reported of a fourth year geography group engaged on a topic which heightened economic awareness:

> The lesson concerned the issue of water use, and was in the form of a case study. The class was divided into four groups, each of which had to prepare a report for a simulated public enquiry on the use of the Great Ouse river, each group to regard itself as a 'special interest group' preparing evidence for the enquiry. The teacher intended to video this event. The groups worked well, each having a strong identification with the interest they were supposed to represent and the issues involved. The group discussions were supported by an excellent range of resources: case study details, relevant data, a study guide and carefully structured notes. There was a high standard of presentation of these materials. The unit identified key concepts and skills to be assessed. There was a strong economics dimension to this lesson and much of its success in both motivating the pupils and increasing their understanding was attributable to appropriate teaching methods in association with effective material.
>
> (DES, 1987, p. 13)

While this was not a lesson specifically designed for children with learning difficulties it contained many aspects which should be incorporated into schemes of work for these children, especially the use of video to record the statements of the group after they had completed their research for the enquiry.

'Active' watching of the video of the children's work can be ensured by involving the children in the assessment process. They can be encouraged to 'mark' the work of other groups, the criteria for marking can be discussed in advance and discussion of what sort of things should be marked can aid the learning process. This approach reinforces stated objectives which have been shared with the children at the beginning of the topic and is an aid to future learning.

Tape recorders

All secondary schools have tape recorders and they are, perhaps, the most common of the hardware available for use with children who have special needs. Although there is no longer the novelty value related to the use of tape recorders, they still have a variety of most positive uses in the classroom.

1. The use by pupils who have difficulty writing for recording their ideas or answers. If it is practical, these can later be typed up by the teacher, the support teacher or the NTA.

Putting ideas directly onto tape cuts out the 'head to hand' dimension of the recording. Many pupils with special needs may have the ideas in their heads. The problems occur when they come to commit their thoughts to paper. If they have the ideas it is incumbent upon teachers to allow them to express them in any way they can. As we have seen, frustration is a major cause of failure and of unwillingness to try again.

2. Tape recorders can be used by pupils when developing a long narrative to a visual stimulus. If teachers are aiming to encourage children to consider carefully a primary source, for example, it may prove productive to allow the thoughts to 'flow' onto tape rather than to record them by writing. Speaking comes more easily to pupils than does writing.

3. In field study situations, it is more immediate to record on tape what is being seen and observed than to make notes or even to remember what has been seen after the event. This is, after all, the technique used by estate agents, social workers and house surveyors. It is a 'real' technique not one which has been especially developed for children with learning difficulties. It is a technique which is useful for all pupils on field trips. Pupils record their observations and thoughts on site and then have their own *aide mémoire* when they return to base.

4. As we have seen, making information accessible to children who find reading difficult is a major problem. When the content of a piece is important and the reading level too difficult it should be possible for the teacher to put the text onto tape for the pupils to hear. This is of particular use in the study of first hand evidence in history when the handwriting of a figure in the past may, in any case, be difficult to follow. In such situations, the original, a type-script, a simplified typescript and a tape should all be available. If tape recorders are to be used in the classroom a headset is important. It is disrupting for a whole class to have to tolerate audible commentaries when it is trying to work on other matters. However, classes will soon become accustomed to the presence of machines which only a minority of the children are using. If some children are using headsets and listening to tapes from the start of the secondary school career, even if this had not been the experience in the primary school, it soon becomes an accepted part of lessons and receives no comment from other children. It is accepted as a natural part of the classroom routine just as in some classes teachers wear

microphones and some children receivers to aid hearing, and in others some children use Alpha vision enlargers to assist their sight.

5. Tape recorders are also useful for children to record answers in social science interviews. Many children are loath to ask people questions in the street if they are unable to write down the answers quickly enough. On the other hand, many find the prospect of interviewing people using a tape recorder much more appealing.

There are, of course, the usual inherent difficulties with using tape recorders. Pushing the wrong button and losing the recorded information, tapes being shredded or snarled up in the machine or batteries running out at the crucial moment are all accidents that have happened to us. Care of the machines and regular checking is important. As far as children are concerned, part of the process of learning is organisational skill and this can be added into the program of teaching objectives for children who have learning difficulties. As a safeguard, though, it is probably best to have a back-up copy of any work staff have recorded to prevent unnecessary irritation if things do go wrong.

Example 6.10
A teacher decided to enlist the help of a small group of third year children with learning difficulties in teaching a first year class. They were going to make a film to demonstrate how to go about a field study. The film was then to be shown to first year children in their humanities lesson. It happened that the area in which this school was sited had a reservoir which had been created and had drowned a village. The task was to research the history of this village now 60 feet beneath the level of the water.

The task took several weeks and produced a film which, after editing, was just 20 minutes long. The process of making the film was full of important and enjoyable learning experiences, even though the product was relatively short.

The children were introduced to the topic and the objectives of the short course were outlined to the group. The teacher had prepared the topic well. She had:

*   produced simple information sheets on making a film;
*   organised people in the area who remembered the village or who knew something about what had happened. They agreed to be interviewed by the children; the teacher, however, did not make precise arrangements, this was to be left to the children.

- booked a school minibus, in advance, for five weeks worth of lessons so that children could go 'on site';
- collected together a whole range of resources which might be of use. These included newspapers recording the event, photographs from the Local Studies library, some artefacts from the local Museum Service that were similar to the sorts of household goods which would have been in the houses before they were evacuated. Where necessary the newspapers were both translated into simplified language and put onto tape.

The motivation of these children improved tremendously. While often seen slouching along the corridors late for lessons, unwilling to make much effort, suddenly they wanted to be early for this teacher's lesson. They volunteered to give up their lunchtime to start their research before the afternoon session began.

The final video was well received by the first years who felt that it was informative and well done, for an amateur enterprise. The third year children were generally congratulated and agreed that the film making had been a very positive experience.

During the course of working on this topic the children had practised many of the essential skills of learning in the humanities:

- Artefacts had been handled and described. They had tried to use this primary evidence to piece together what life might have been like in the village. By doing this they were able to understand something of continuity and change in their local area.
- Skills of observation and recording had been used by going to the site and noticing where the reservoir was and where the position of the village had been.
- Some mapwork had been done. The planning office had provided the plans of the village before its drowning and the children had used these and made simplified versions of their own.
- Some mathematical work had been employed. They had obtained the census returns for the last census before the valley was flooded and from these they were able to estimate how many people had lived there.
- In certain cases some family history was studied. Two of the children found that some of their ancestors had lived in the village which set them off on another line of enquiry.
- Some physical geography had been done. They were able to approach the water board and discover why the valley had been chosen as one worth flooding and discovered something of rock patterns in their local area.

- Through their contact with the water board they had begun to understand something of the economics of the water industry.

These were skills directly related to humanities subjects; they had additionally practised other skills.

- They had been working together; many of these children did not find mixing easy. Some still found it difficult at the end of this course of study but others were better able to work with their peers at the end of the topic.
- The project had involved language work. They had spoken into a camera, prepared written scripts which they then read, and interviewed people face to face.

The benefits of this course were enormous for most of the children concerned. Through humanities their self esteem had improved, their social confidence was greater, their motivation strengthened, and their understanding and knowledge greatly improved. As the teacher intended the making of the film was largely irrelevant: it was merely a focus, a force for motivation and a spur to positive learning. The teacher had designed a skills matrix in advance, listing those skills she wanted each child to practise. For each child this grid sheet was ticked when appropriate to ensure that, individually, the children were receiving a range of experiences. At each stage the objectives and the reasons for the activity were shared in the way set out in Chapter 4. As such the project was hugely successful.

REFERENCES

Allen, H. (1982) 'History trails'. In McIver, V. (ed.) *Teaching History to Slow Learning Children in Secondary Schools*. Belfast: Learning Resources Unit.

Arkell, T. (1982) How do readability tests detect difficulties in History texts? *Teaching History*, **32**.

Boardman, D. (1982) 'Assessing readability'. In Boardman, D. (ed.) *Geography and Slow Learners*. Sheffield: The Geographical Association.

Brennan, W. (1979) *The Curricular Needs of Slow Learners*. Schools Council Working Paper 63. London: Evans/Methuen Educational.

Bullock Report (1975) *Language for Life. Report of the Committee of Enquiry*. London: HMSO.

Cavan, D. (1982) 'Methods of assisting with the teaching of reading in the history class' In McIver, V. (ed.) *Teaching History to Slow Learning Children in Secondary Schools*. Belfast: Learning Resource Unit.

Dyke, R. G. (1986) *Supporting the Low Attainer – the Power of the Micro-computer*. Microelectronics Education Programme.

Fay, A. and Fay, J. P. (1982) 'CAL activities in Irish history classrooms'. In McIver, V. (ed.) *Teaching History to Slow Learning Children in the Secondary School*. Belfast: Learning Resource Unit.

Hagerty, J. and Hill, M. History and less able children. *Teaching History*, **30**, pp. 19–23.

Harrison, C. (1980) *Readability in the Classroom*. Cambridge University Press.

DES (1982) *Report of the Committee of Inquiry into the Teaching of Mathematics in Schools* (The Cockcroft Report). London: HMSO.

DES (1987) *HMI Report on Economic Awareness*. London: HMSO.

Kinlock, N. (1985) '1914 – the making of a computer simulation'. In Wilkes, J. (ed.) *Exploring History with Micro-computers*. Leicester: H. Cave.

Kintsch, W. (1974) *The Representation of Meaning in Memory*. New Jersey: Hillsdale.

Lunzer, E. and Gardner, K. (eds) (1979) *The Effective Use of Reading*. London: Heinemann.

Martin, K. (1987) 'Secondary school support and content free software'. In *Manchester SEMERC Newsletter*. Spring.

McCleod, P. (1981) *A Place to Work*. London: Hutchinson.

Rea, F. (1985) 'Computer assisted learning in primary school history'. In Wilkes, J. (ed.) *Exploring History with Micro Computers*. Leicester: H. Cave.

Sayer, J. (1987) *Secondary Schools for All? Strategies for Special Needs*. London: Cassell.

Schools Council (1982) *Reading for Learning in the Secondary School*. London: Methuen Educational.

Smith, M. G. (1985) 'From mainframe to micro'. In Wilkes, J. (ed.) *Exploring History with Micro Computers*. Leicester: H. Cave.

Warn, C. (1986) *Ordnance Survey Map Skills Book*. Arnold-Wheaton and Ordnance Survey.

Weber, K. J. (1978) *Yes They Can! A Practical Guide for Teaching the Adolescent Slow Learner*. Oxford: Oxford University Press.

Wilson, M. D. (1985) *History for Children with Learning Difficulties*. London: Hodder and Stoughton.

Ideas for INSET

Rather than give a conventional summary in this last chapter we will provide some guidelines for Inservice Training which incorporate most of the main points made in earlier chapters. The teachers' new contract, new funding arrangements, and the planned introduction of a system of appraisal all imply more opportunities for INSET. Inservice training in humanities for children with learning difficulties could take a variety of forms, from LEA organised courses to school focused sessions organised by heads of department either for their own departments or for those of two or three schools. These comments will be sensitive to the variety of arrangements which are possible, although primarily they are aimed at those wishing to organise school-focused and school-based INSET.

Anyone who is engaged in organising INSET should bear the following points in mind which are covered in more detail in the INSET literature (e.g. Easen, 1985, relating to mainstream; Robson et al., 1988, relating to special educational needs):

1. Have the needs of teachers been identified? Do the teachers you intend to work with perceive that there is a need to discuss and possibly change their practice?

    This will be made much easier if there is a commitment towards special needs by the senior management of the school and if there is a development towards a whole-school policy. If neither of these conditions exist, the job is more difficult. In this case, perhaps the best strategy heads of departments can adopt is to seek the support of their LEA adviser. Additionally they should identify colleagues who seem keen and secure their support. Thirdly they could produce short discussion documents for the consideration of their departments. These may initially centre on entirely practical issues such as setting out the alternative strategies for teaching a particular group of students or an individual student. Out of this, teachers may perceive that further discussion of the general issues could be worth while.

    Above all else heads of department should be positive and encouraging. Children with learning difficulties are often difficult to teach and if heads of department can present their proposed INSET in terms of a strategy which would improve pupil motivation and performance and make them easier to teach, teacher interest is likely to be higher. Teachers need to feel that their time is being used for their benefit.

2. The design of the course should incorporate clear objectives. Teachers should know clearly what the course is trying to do, not merely in global terms but also in terms of individual sessions. If the course is being offered to a group of schools then the initial approaches should make it absolutely clear what the course intends to do and at whom it is aimed. Ideally, if teachers from other schools are attending then there should be at least two from each. It is often suggested that it is extremely difficult to bring about change in a school if only one person is fully aware of what that change is to be. Two teachers, working in concert, have a much better chance. Moreover, should one teacher leave, there is another to carry on the work.

3. In considering the implementation of course aims, course leaders should ensure that the objectives are reflected in the manner of delivery. If the course intends, for example, to encourage teachers to consider the uses to which the micro-processor can be put, then course participants should be working with the machines. If the course wishes to encourage group work strategies with children who have learning difficulties then this should be reflected in the course. Much of the learning which takes place on the course should come through group work and not through a lecture format.

4. The course needs to be evaluated. Evaluation has been built into the Grant Related Inservice Training arrangements (GRIST) and there has been a growing concern as to the effectiveness of INSET. The essential point of evaluation is to discover how many of the course objectives have been reached and, in addition, how much of what is learned is carried into schools. The evaluation should make clear what, if any, changes in classroom and departmental practice have come about as the result of the INSET and should point to cases where there has, for example, been innovation but no real change.

The great advantage of school-based, school-focused courses is that there is a much greater chance of change following the INSET. If discussions have centred on practical problems within the classroom, such as the development of resources or teaching strategies for children with learning difficulties, or on departmental problems, such as the rôle which is to be played by support teachers, there is a much higher chance of success. If some possible solutions have been generally agreed and a general departmental policy on special needs has been adopted, those solutions and that policy can be continually evaluated within the department. Not everything which has been discussed as a possible solution to problems will work. There may be timetabling constraints or problems of personnel which lead certain strategies to fail. In this case further meetings may discuss and change these strategies so that something else is tried. This is the continual process of departmental development.

The following model of departmental development is the same as that used in the development of courses for students with learning difficulties:

1. Set objectives.
   - Decide what the department aims to do.
   - Are the objectives 'real, relevant, rational, and realistic'?
   - How will the department know when the objectives have been reached?
2. Decide on method.
   - How does the department intend to achieve the objectives?
   - Has the department applied the 'Principle of Parsimony' – i.e. has it worked on the basis of minimum intervention – is it intending to try the most simple strategy first?
3. Evaluate.
   - Have the objectives been reached?
   - If not, why not?
4. Change method.
   - Try something else.
5. Evaluate.
   - Have the objectives been reached?
   - If not, why not?
   - Is there something wrong with the objectives?
   - Do we need to change something which is beyond our control, e.g. the timetable, the system of banding or setting in the school, the attitude of the special needs department?

INSET activities

The following outline some ideas which can be developed either as individual sessions or as part of a longer course.

Activity 1 – setting objectives (1)

Begin this process by describing the essence of the objectives-based approach, specifically the five criteria of
reality
relevance
realism
rationality
operationalism (see Chapter 4).

Distribute copies of an individual lesson plan, lesson notes, and resources used. In groups, the course participants analyse the lesson in terms of these criteria and make judgements as to its appropriateness for children with learning difficulties. They then design a lesson on the same humanities topic which might be considered to be more appropriate for children with learning difficulties. A further exercise is to set the groups the tasks of working out an appropriate way of assessing whether the objectives have been reached and an efficient way of recording the assessments.

As with many exercises of this type the group work is crucial to the exercise for it is here that teachers begin to appreciate that others have the same fears and difficulties as they have. It is in group sessions like this that the real learning takes place.

Activity 2 – setting objectives (2)

This is similar to 1, but in this case course participants are asked to analyse not a lesson plan but a computer program. They are asked to play the simulation game (possibly the 'Viking Raiders', or 'Fletcher's Castle', or the 'Fishing Game') and then, in groups of three or four list

- what pre skills are required;
- the teaching objectives which might be set for children with learning difficulties using this software;
- any extra resources which children with learning difficulties might need in order to work more effectively with the software (Chapter 4).

This works well with groups of teachers who may not be familiar with the micro as a teaching aid. Additionally it builds on Activity 1 in its concentration on the Objectives Approach.

Activity 3 – setting objectives (3)

The process of learning about objectives is extended to include a whole humanities topic. Perhaps a useful starting point is McCall's

(1982) example (see chapter 4) regarding the British in India. This explains how a whole teaching unit can be envisaged in terms of objectives. If teachers have been asked to bring one of their own schemes of work or syllabus topics, they can work on this. Otherwise the course leader should provide a variety of topics for teachers to work on. Equally, this is something which teachers may be asked to do between sessions and then to discuss their ideas at the next.

Activity 4 – task analysis

The course leader explains the basic process of task analysis (Chapter 4). Some of the groups of course participants then task analyse the skill of the tying of a shoelace. The other groups task analyse the skill of tying a necktie. They write down the steps in their analysis. When each group has completed its written analysis it tries either to tie a shoelace or a necktie using only the instructions given to it by the other groups. In sessions with small groups of people it might be more appropriate for all the participants to watch while the steps are read out and someone tries to tie the tie or shoelace from the instructions. This is a lively way to bring home the message that task analysis is useful but that it must be done carefully or great confusion results.

The course participants are then introduced to the process of task analysis as an aid to teaching. They are asked, in their groups, to task analyse something in humanities teaching (see the example on Grid Reference in Chapter 4). It is important to be sensitive here to the background of the participants. Many would prefer to practise these techniques with topics from their own discipline. It might be useful to have a series of tasks for analysis from the various disciplines which make up the humanities.

Activity 5 – readability

This is an activity which is easy to organise. Teachers are asked to bring along a written information sheet which they have designed or they are provided with one. They are asked to analyse its reading level, hopefully using a computer program (see Chapter 6). Their task, then, working in groups of two or three, is to rewrite the piece so that it is easier to read. They then test their new piece to see what effect their changes have had.

This is followed by a general discussion of the merits of readability tests and discussion of what other factors make a piece easier for children with learning difficulties to read apart from its reading level. Many of the issues likely to be explored here are to be found in Chapter 5.

Activity 6 – oral work

This activity combines work on language with the use of video film. After a general introduction about language (see Chapter 5) teachers are asked to watch a section of a video recorded TV programme (about 15 minutes long) and note the changes of language which the soundtrack would need to make it intelligible to the children with learning difficulties taught by them.

In groups they compare the results of this work and discuss why they thought that something would not be comprehended. This is followed by a discussion as to ways in which the same video could be used with language which was more accessible. Discussion of other strategies, e.g. class discussion and the explanation of key words would also be appropriate here.

The final discussion would centre round the problems of the language which teachers use. Some course participants need to have been persuaded in advance to have a lesson they had delivered taped or video recorded. Choice of teachers who are self confident is crucial for this and they must be willing participants. Failing that, course leaders who are teachers should expose themselves to pedagogic criticism by taping one of their own lessons. If they fail to do this their credibility as course leaders is brought into question. An alternative is to write a 'transcript' of an imaginary lesson bringing out the main point as to how some language confuses students. This would lead to a general discussion of strategies which teachers can adopt to lessen the use of inappropriate language.

Activity 7 – video making

The purpose of this activity is to encourage the course participants to consider the benefits of making video films with children. The course leaders would identify a local issue or field site which could be used for this exercise and ask the participants, working in groups of four or five to design a teaching unit around the making of a video.

They should be encouraged to consider objectives, other resources and to gauge the number of positive learning outcomes which they believe the use of video would create. There are suggestions on this in Chapter 6, but this is not an exhaustive list and teachers should be encouraged to produce their own ideas.

Activity 8 – use of support teachers

This activity aims to encourage course participants to develop productive strategies for using an extra teacher, or other adult, in the classroom. It is best to begin by using the complaints of some support teachers who work in mainstream classes in the form of quotes. For example, course participants can be given a list:

- I feel left out;
- I feel like a second-class teacher;
- The kids say 'Here comes the Thickies' teacher';
- I never know anything about the lesson before I get there;
- I don't understand what I'm supposed to be doing.
- I think the class teacher thinks I'm just there to spy for the deputy head;
- I'm not very confident because I don't understand what these humanities lessons are all about. I thought it was just going to be ox bow lakes and king and queens.

The course participants then have the task of working out a sensible policy for a humanities department which would govern their relations with support teachers. They work in groups and write a departmental policy statement. The statements are prepared and ideas collated in a plenary session. Although suggestions appear in this book (especially in Chapter 5) about how support teachers may be used, it is important to remember that their rôle will vary from school to school and that there are no precise guidelines which can be laid down. Working in groups in this way, course participants should come to their solutions to problems and in that way feel some 'ownership' of the policy which eventually emerges in their school.

Activity 9 – teacher style

This activity should be left until near the end of any sessions since, potentially, it is the most threatening to teachers. The course leaders produce some examples of practice which do nothing except destroy the motivation of children who have learning difficulties. These take the form of imaginary pages from exercise books and transcripts from imaginary lessons. They are given an imaginary case study of a child that includes school reports, notes to heads of year about behaviour, and letters to parents about lack of effort.

The task is to consider whether the school has any responsibility for creating or compounding the child's difficulties. It is to develop the idea of teacher style as being a crucial element in the attitude of a student to lessons. Again the task is performed in groups.

This activity does not have any direct application for humanities teaching specifically but it is important for teachers interested in developing a whole-school policy towards special educational needs. Teachers who have worked on the activities detailed above may well, in their own schools, find that the general atmosphere and structure militates against the development of a policy which will meet the needs of all children. As such, they will need a wider picture than simply humanities teaching will give them. An activity like this one can begin the process which leads to a wider view. Further examples can be found in *Special Needs in the Secondary School* (Ainscow and Muncey, 1987) which is a collection of course materials, and addresses the issues in an unambiguous manner.

CONCLUSION

It has been our contention throughout this book that children with learning difficulties have been neglected in humanities lessons. We have argued that to teach such children requires skills in excess of those required to teach the high achievers. We hope, during its course, to have given a philosophic framework within which humanities teachers may work. We hope to have offered practical help to teachers faced, daily, with the task of teaching pupils who do not find learning easy. We believe that the adoption of this teaching model and the use of some of these teaching strategies will have great benefit not only for children with learning difficulties and their teachers but also for the general school population. As teachers begin to concentrate more on the needs of some children the change in atmosphere is to the advantage of all.

REFERENCES

Ainscow, M. and Muncey, J. (1987) *Special Needs in the Secondary School (Special Needs Action Project)*. Cardiff: Drake.

Easen, P. (1985) *Making School-Centred INSET Work*. London: Croom Helm and Open University Press.

McCall, C. (1982) 'Some national reports and surveys: implications for the remedial specialist'. In Hinson, M. and Hughes, M. *Planning Effective Progress*. Amersham: Hulton Educational.

Robson, C., Sebba, J., Mittler, P. and Davies, G. (1988) *In-Service Training and Special Educational Needs: Running Short, School Focused Courses*. Manchester: Manchester University Press.

Further reading

These books and articles are in addition to the references at the end of each chapter.

Ainscow, M. and Tweddle, D. (1979) *Preventing Classroom Failure: An Objectives Approach*. Chichester: Wiley.

Ainscow, M. and Muncey, J. (1981) *Small Steps: A Workshop Guide about Teaching Children with Learning Difficulties*. Coventry LEA.

Boardman, D. (ed.) (1982) *Geography with Slow Learners*. Sheffield: The Geographical Association.

Clunies-Ross, L. and Wimhurst, S. (1983) *The Right Balance: Provision for Slow Learners in Secondary Schools*. Windsor: NFER/Nelson.

Corney, G. and Rawling, E. (eds) (1985) *Teaching Slow Learners through Geography*. Sheffield: The Geographical Association.

Cornwall, K. F. (1981) Some trends in pupil evaluation: the growing importance of the teacher's role. *Remedial Education*, 16 (4).

Galletley, I. (1976) How to do away with yourself. *Remedial Education*, 15 (1), pp. 5–9.

Hinson, M. and Hughes, M. (eds) (1982) *Planning Effective Progress*. Amersham: Hulton Educational.

Hodgson, A., Clunies-Ross, L. and Hegarty, S. (1984) *Learning Together: Teaching Pupils with Special Educational Needs in the Ordinary School*. Windsor: NFER.

Hodkinson, P. (1977) Mixed ability teaching: how can we choose appropriate techniques? *Teaching Geography*, 12 (3), pp. 108–109.

Hull, J. (1980) Practical points in teaching history to less able secondary pupils. *Teaching History*, 26, pp. 14–16.

Kemp, R. (1979) Teaching strategies for the less able. *Teaching Geography*, 52.

Keogh, B. K. (1975) 'Social and ethical assumptions about special education'. In Wedell, K. (ed.) *Orientation in Special Education*. London: Wiley.

Lovitt, T. C. (1977) *In Spite of my Resistance I've Learned from my Children*. Columbus: Merrill.

Mills, D. (ed.) (1981) *Geographical Work in Primary and Middle Schools*. Sheffield: The Geographical Association.

Smith, C. J. (ed.) (1986) *New Directions in Remedial Education*. London: The Falmer Press.

Visser, J. (1986) Support: a description of the work of the SEN professional. *Support for Learning*, 1 (4).

Name Index

Subject Index